THE NEW COMPLETE
Chesapeake Bay Retriever

Chesapeake Bay Retriever. *R. Ward Binks*. Provenance: Mrs. Geraldine Rockefeller Dodge, commission. St. Hubert's Giralda Animal Welfare and Education Center. Courtesy William Secord Gallery, New York.

THE NEW COMPLETE
Chesapeake Bay Retriever

Janet Horn
and
Dr. Daniel Horn

HOWELL
BOOK HOUSE

New York

Howell Book House
Macmillan General Reference
A Simon & Schuster Macmillan Company
1633 Broadway
New York, NY 10019-6785

Library of Congress Cataloging-in-Publication Data

Horn, Janet.
    The new complete Chesapeake Bay retriever / by Janet Horn and
Dr. Daniel Horn.
        p.   cm.
    Includes bibliographical references (p.   ).
    ISBN 0-87605-099-2
    1. Chesapeake Bay retrievers. I. Horn, Daniel, 1916—
II. Title.   III. Title: Complete Chesapeake Bay retriever.
SF429.C4H67 1994   93-6340   CIP
636.7'52—dc20

10 9 8 7 6 5 4

Printed in the United States of America

To "Breakers,"
who gave us his all,
and to "Keeper,"
who keeps on giving

Ch. Barnum retrieving at Carroll's Island Gun Club. From a painting by J. M. Tracy. Barnum was the first AKC Champion Chesapeake.

Contents

Foreword

The Chesapeake Bay Retriever was named for the famous bay where the breed originated and it is one of the few breeds actually developed in the United States. Many articles have been published about these unique dogs but only a very few books have been written exclusively about the Chesapeake Bay Retriever. Now drawing on her many years of experience with these dogs, Janet Horn has produced a book that covers a wide variety of subjects, starting with the era of Sailor and Canton in the breed's early history, right up to the present time.

These extremely versatile dogs are accomplished in many areas besides the field and water work they are so famous for. In addition to being matchless companions and devoted family dogs, they also excel in competing at dog shows and Obedience Trials, working with drug enforcement agencies, as service dogs, helping people with hearing impairments, and visiting nursing homes, hospitals and psychiatric facilities. Some are trained for Search and Rescue work or as Avalanche dogs while still others have been trained as sled dogs. The list of their abilities and achievements seems endless.

Whether you are someone who wants to know more about the Chesapeake, a novice owner or the long time devotee of the breed, this book has something for everyone. Janet Horn is a talented writer, well versed in her subject, who has created a book that is informative as well as entertaining reading for all.

Thank you, Janet.

Lorraine Berg

Acknowledgments

I wish to thank the many friends who have contributed so much to the contents of this book. Lorraine Berg and I have known each other since she and her husband, Ray, first began to show their Cheasapeakes to championship and Obedience titles in the early 1960s. Shortly afterward, the Bergs founded Chesapine Kennels. During the years when they were most active and successful in shows, their dogs continued to excel in hunting as they do today. They have worked for the breed and served the Parent Club in several capacities over the years. Most recently Lorraine Berg has been president of the American Chesapeake Club. To encourage conformation quality and working ability, the Bergs offer annually the Chesapine Trophy, a wooden duck drake hand-carved out of basswood, to a Chesapeake earning both a bench championship and a Field Champion or a Master Hunter title.

Next, the breeder-judges who answered my call to put into words their mental processes in judging the breed by its Standard as they officiate in the ring: William K. Boyson, Mildred Buchholz, Edith Hanson, Nathaniel Horn and Elizabeth Humer. The article on coat by Daniel Horn was found among his papers and is one of the few pieces actually written and brought to completion by him to be available for this book.

Millie Buchholz's understanding of Chesapeakes inspired the new chapter on Teaching the Chesapeake Puppy, and we could not do better than her chapter on Tracking.

Les Lowenthal has honored this book with his excellent chapter on the Hunting Retriever Tests, in which he has been active since their inception, and has served in advisory capacities in the development of these Tests by the American Kennel Club.

Nat Horn, a conformation exhibitor to the point of addiction, has studied in depth the imponderables and variables of the sport of showing dogs, and his discussion is especially valuable to the owner-handler who has the courage to compete with professionals at all levels of showing.

Sarah Horn, my granddaughter, is well qualified to write about Junior Showmanship, a facet of showing dogs which is deserving of increasing respect. This is well attested to by the excellent material she has contributed.

Dyane Baldwin wrote on Grooming, and we could not do better than to reprint her work from the American Kennel Gazette. This is only the ''tip of the iceberg,'' for Dyane's contributions have been so many and so varied that I cannot identify them except to say they came in relating to all aspects of the breed and expecially augmenting the historical background material.

Betsy Humer contributed the section on Obedience, and Betsy and I both thank Susan Cone for her personal account of ''Abby,'' the first Chesapeake Obedience Trial Champion. The help that Betsy has given me cannot be measured; her contributions have been many and varied and absolutely essential to the production of this book.

Sally Diess's chapter on training for the Tracking Dog Excellent is another that breaks new ground, and Sally is not only exceptionally well qualified to deal with the subject, her exposition is a clear and competent guide to the TDX, and we are fortunate in being able to publish it.

For the new material in the chapter on Chesapeakes Abroad, we must thank Christine Mayhew (the former Lady Spencer-Smith) for a comprehensive account of progress the breed has made in the United Kingdom; Birgitte Jorgenssen, a new and diligent worker for the breed in Denmark; Marianne Nilsson Johansson, one of my oldest friends in Sweden and Catharina Lindstrom, who also welcomed us to Grycksbo in 1979, for their separate reports on developments in Sweden; Gun Holmström, the first importer and still the leading breeder in Finland; Maya Mächler whose activity with the breed in Switzerland is only equalled by her devotion to it; Audrey Austin, who has witnessed the first manifestations of the Chesapeake breed in Germany, and Benedetta Gilardini, who has had the unique experience of introducing the Chesapeake Bay Retriever into Italy.

Thanks are due and I am grateful to people too numerous to name, who sent me photographs and other illustrative material and useful and interesting information in correspondence.

I wish also to thank Caroline Humer for technical assistance that was invaluable to me. Currently in graduate school at Columbia University, Caroline has made publishing, writing and editing her profession, and her gift for organization provided solid ground for my endeavors, enhanced by her knowledge of the material.

Special Acknowledgment

Eloise Heller Cherry was one of the dearest of the many friends that Chesapeakes have made for me. In revising her book, *The Complete Chesapeake Bay Retriever*, she lived again for me. No one, I felt, could better explain Field Trials and her deep feeling for them. It was my desire to republish her chapters on her favorite aspect of the sport of dogs. In other chapters her expression of beliefs and principles could not have been bettered, and as I introduced enhancements but not alterations, these chapters became almost collaborations which I felt would have met with her approval. I have felt very close to Eloise throughout the writing of this book. I am grateful for all that she did for the breed we both loved, and cannot express by gratitude for the privilege of having been her friend.

CHESAPEAKE
BAY RETRIEVER
AMERICAS ONLY NATIVE BRED HUNTING DOG
HUNTING DOGS
FIELD TRIAL DOGS
FAMILY DOGS
COMPANION DOGS
THERE IS NO BETTER ALL-ROUND DOG

Introduction

This book was conceived as a joint project for my husband and myself, a kind of culmination of our love for Chesapeakes and our long association with this breed. In 1933 in an apartment in Cambridge, Massachusetts, the home of a college classmate, I found an old, yet very beautiful dog. On enquiry I was told that he was a Chesapeake Bay Retriever. I had never before heard of this breed, and for me it was love at first sight. I was entranced when the old gentleman, aloof yet courteous, graciously permitted me to pet him.

A few years later, spending the first summer of our marriage in Maine, we found a summer visitor from Philadelphia next door, or perhaps he found us, for he sought our companionship, waited patiently for us to come out of our house, was delighted to retrieve whatever we would throw for him and happily joined us on long walks into the country. He seemed to enjoy sharing our simple recreations as much as we enjoyed him. His name was Rusty and he was a young dog of perhaps two or three years. As our acquaintance with Chesapeake character began with him, we resolved that someday we would have a Chesapeake of our own. World War II intervened, and it was nearly ten years later, on our return to civilian life, that my husband surprised me on my birthday with a gift of a Chesapeake puppy: the best birthday present I ever had.

My husband used to say, "I like Chesapeakes because they do smart things." Intelligence, initiative and ability to solve problems are theirs to a marked degree, and life with a Chesapeake is never dull. Our first Chesapeake took her place as a member of our family, and changed our lives, for by falling in love with her we fell in love with the whole wonderful breed. Our children grew up with Chesapeakes, and as we raised our Chesapeakes along with raising our children, the dogs were always part of our family.

Some of the many things we learned from and through our dogs and some of the ways in which Chesapeakes have enriched our lives, I have tried to show in this book. The Chesapeake is not a breed for everyone; for some their demonstrations of love and loyalty may seem burdensome, but for those who are attuned to this rare perceptivity and depth of devotion, there is no other dog.

1

Chesapeake Origin
and History

THE FULL HISTORY of the development of the Chesapeake Bay Retriever can never be known. It is certain that for more than two centuries dogs have been used on the Chesapeake Bay to recover the waterfowl that were shot down, formerly in great numbers, especially during the migration of huge flocks in the winter season, often when the weather was stormy and very cold. The dog for this work must love water, birds and retrieving and must be physically strong and able to resist extremes of temperature and rough, icy waters. It was reported in 1739 that, on the Chesapeake Bay, "the shooting of waterfowl is performed . . . with a water spaniel."

All stories of the beginnings of the retriever breeds seem to hark back to a water spaniel unlike any spaniel we know today. Crosses with hounds, setters, Newfoundlands and others were made. The special attributes of the Chesapeake Bay dog derive from two Newfoundland puppies rescued from a shipwreck in the year 1807, whose superior qualities resulted in improvement of whatever local ducking dogs were bred to them, and it seems safe to assume that some of these were descendants of the water spaniel of sixty years earlier. In those days such dogs were bred for a purpose, not for profit. Among landowners the owning and breeding of livestock was as much a part of life as it was for

This woodcut of early retrievers shows that breeds were often mixed. Left, Water Spaniel–Setter cross. Right, Setter-Newfoundland cross. Rear dog, Water Spaniel–Newfoundland cross.—*Retriever International*

their English forebears; they were sportsmen and valued highly the dogs that made "ducking" supreme among the sports of the Chesapeake Bay area. These men sought to acquire and to produce good ducking dogs, applying their knowledge of conformation, management and the principles of breeding quality stock.

The romantic concept of the Chesapeake dog as a spontaneous product in the rugged life of the bay men, with all the charm of the "Noble Savage" as envisioned by Jean-Jacques Rousseau of the same period has proved attractive to some admirers of the breed, but no true breed of the Chesapeake's distinctive type and character could have been established in a haphazard fashion, and it is necessary to acknowledge the debt owed to the dedicated and creative breeders who succeeded in establishing bloodlines and recognizable strains through planned and thoughtful breeding over a period of years. The breeding of these dogs was often "handed down" in a family from one generation to the next, each continuing the original strain while seeking to maintain and improve its quality. These dogs were part of the family life of their breeders and shared in the many activities of their busy, beautiful country homes.

The Chesapeake Bay dog was the greatest meat dog the waterman and market gunner ever had, and for the leading citizens of Baltimore and the surrounding countryside it was the only dog capable of honorably sharing their favorite sport, bred by them according to the concept of an animal of the highest physical and mental character as dictated by the same good taste shown in the landscaping and furnishing of their dwelling places.

The Dog, by William Youatt, was first published in 1846, and states, "the water-spaniel was originally from Spain; but the pure breed has been lost, and the present dog is probably descended from the large water-dog and the English setter." Youatt classified the Newfoundland as "a spaniel of large size . . . faithful, good-natured and ever friendly to man. They will defend their master and their master's property, and suffer no person to injure either the one or the other; . . . they seem only to want the faculty of speech, and they are capable of being trained for all the purposes for which every other variety of the canine species is used." Youatt quotes an English writer: "As a retriever, the Newfoundland dog is easily brought to do almost anything that is required of him . . . and he may be safely taken among pointers to the field, with whose province he will not interfere, but will be overjoyed to be allowed to look up the wounded game . . . and he never shines more than when he is returning with a woodcock, pheasant or hare, in his mouth, which he yields up, or even puts into your hand unmutilated." T. S. Skinner, in *The Dog and the*

Sportsman, published in 1845, documents the accidental introduction of this breed into the Chesapeake Bay area through the following letter:

Baltimore, Maryland
January 7th, 1845.

My Dear Sir;—In the fall of 1807 I was on board of the ship Canton, belonging to my uncle, the late Hugh Thompson, of Baltimore, when we fell in, at sea, near the termination of a very heavy equinoctial gale, with an English brig in a sinking condition, and took off the crew. The brig was loaded with codfish, and was bound to Poole, England, from Newfoundland.

I boarded her, in command of a boat from the Canton, which was sent to take off the English crew, the brig's own boats having been all swept away, and her crew in a state of intoxication.

I found on board of her two Newfoundland pups, male and female, which I saved, and subsequently, on our landing the English crew at Norfolk, our own destination being Baltimore, I purchased these two pups of the English captain for a guinea a-piece.

Being bound again to sea, I gave the dog-pup, which was called Sailor, to Mr. John Mercer, of West River; and the slut-pup, which was called Canton, to Doctor James Stewart, of Sparrow's Point.

The history the English captain gave me of these pups was, that the owner of his brig was extensively engaged in the Newfoundland trade, and had directed his correspondent to select and send him a pair of pups of the most approved Newfoundland breed, but of different families, and that the pair I purchased of him were selected under this order. The dog was of a dingy red colour, and the slut black. They were not large; their hair was short, but very thick coated; they had dew claws.

Both attained great reputation as water-dogs. They were most sagacious in everything, particularly so in all duties connected with duck-shooting.

Governor Lloyd exchanged a Mexican ram for the dog at the time of the merino fever, when such rams were selling for many hundred dollars, and took him over to his estate on the eastern shore of Maryland, where his progeny were well known for many years after, and may still be known there, and on the western shore, as the Sailor breed.

The slut remained at Sparrow's Point till her death, and her progeny were, and are still, well known through Patapsco Neck, on the Gunpowder, and up the bay, amongst the duck-shooters, as unsurpassed for their purposes.

I have heaard both Doctor Stewart and Mr. Mercer relate most extraordinary instances of the sagacity and performances of both dog and slut, and would refer you to their friends for such particulars as I am unable, at this distance of time to recollect with sufficient accuracy to repeat

Yours, in haste,
GEORGE LAW.

Mr. Skinner made inquiries of Mr. Mercer and of Dr. Stewart, and found "it is ascertained of the former, who owned Sailor, that he was of fine size and figure—lofty in his carriage and built for strength and activity; remarkably muscular and broad across the hips and breast; head large, but not out of proportion; muzzle rather larger than is common with that race of dog; his color a dingy red, with some white on the face and breast; his coat short and smooth, but uncommonly thick, and more like a coarse fur than hair; tail full with long hair, and always carried very high. His eyes were very peculiar; they were so light as to have almost an unnatural appearance, and it is remarkable that in a visit which I made to the eastern shore, nearly twenty years after he was sent there, in a sloop which had been sent expressly for him, to West River, by Governor Lloyd, I saw many of his descendants who were marked with this peculiarity." Canton performed many most extraordinary feats at Sparrows Point: fights with wounded swans, after pursuing them in the water for miles; extraordinary pursuits of wounded ducks, amongst rotten and floating ice, and sometimes in fogs and darkness. "When she was most fatigued, she climbed on a cake of floating ice, and after resting herself on it, she renewed her pursuit of the ducks."

It is not known that Sailor and Canton were ever bred to each other. Although there is a suggestion that this may have occurred, it has long been accepted that Sailor was the progenitor of ducking dogs on the eastern shore, and Canton's great qualities were perpetuated in the dogs used for this purpose on the western shore of the bay. Skinner wrote, "In their descendants, even to the present remote generation, the fine qualities of the original pair are conspicuously preserved, in spite of occasional strains of inferior blood."

FIRST RECOGNITION

Seventy years after their arrival in this country, the astonishly similar progeny of both the eastern and western shore dogs were brought together when a class of Chesapeake Bay ducking dogs was shown for the first time, at the Poultry and Fanciers Association Show, in Baltimore. Their likeness to one another was sufficient to permit the distinct breed of the Chesapeake Bay dog to be recognized.

About thirty sportsmen met to answer the question, could the Chesapeake Bay ducking dog be called a breed "as it originated in a cross, and whether a similar species and color of dog could be reproduced every time?" The meeting adjourned with the appointment of a committee to establish standards and classes for the Chesapeake Bay ducking dog. The committee recognized the breed and divided it into three classes: the otter dog, a tawny sedge color with wavy brown hair, the curly dog and the straight-haired dog, both of a red-brown color. This was the first Standard for the breed, although a decade later Jay Towner, whose kennels were on the Bush River, stated, "They are not bred to any Standard."

The National American Kennel Club was founded in Chicago in 1876, with permanent headquarters in St. Louis. In 1879 it published a Stud Book Register, and the first Chesapeake Bay dog recorded was registered in 1878: Sunday, a male bred by O. D. Foulks and owned by G. E. Keirstead of LaPorte, Indiana. In 1884 the American Kennel Club was organized and was open to registration of Chesapeake Bay dogs from its beginning. Both of these gentlemen contributed many informative articles about this breed to *The American Field* and *The American Sportsman*.

The family of O. D. Foulks had purchased a dog "of the straight-hair class" in 1825, known at the head of the Bay as the "Red Winchester," and bred by several landed individuals along the Bohemia River. Although, as a consequence of the Civil War, Mr. Foulks found the breed to be "fast going out of existence," he had carried on the family strain and was breeding the Winchester fifty years after the acquisition of the first one.

The "otter breed," as described, has many characteristics that would point to it as the principal influence in the development of the breed today; it appears to have been much used in the breeding programs of the gun clubs on the western shore of the Bay, where for a time it was called "the Gunpowder River Dog." Much of the development of a breed of uniform type with distinctive characteristics, a blending of the three types identified above, took place in the last quarter of the nineteenth century in this area under the direction of such men as General Ferdinand C. Latrobe, mayor of Baltimore and head of the Carroll Island kennels, and others who formed the Baltimore Chesapeake Bay Dog Club. This club laid down a Standard for the Chesapeake Bay dog in 1890.

With the decline in numbers of waterfowl in the early years of this century the activities of Maryland breeders were greatly curtailed, but the fame of their dog had spread to the West and to Canada, where the breeders tended to adapt it to the working conditions peculiar to their area. By the time the American Chesapeake Club was founded in 1918 by Earl Henry of Albert Lea, Minnesota, the Chesapeake had truly become an American breed, known and used by waterfowlers everywhere on the North American continent. The American Chesapeake Club became the parent club and its Standard was approved by the American Kennel Club.

6

"FRITZ" DOUGLAS, ALASKA 1921

This reissue of an old postcard speaks for itself.

BREEDING TO A STANDARD

The Standard adopted in 1918 was drawn up by Earl Henry, W. H. Orr and F. E. Richmond, and approved by over fifty breeders in the United States and Canada. Among midwestern breeders were Barron and Orr, of Mason City, Iowa, and Father Joseph Schuster of Onaka, South

Dakota, who registered his dogs with the prefix of Sioux Mission. An early West Coast breeder was William Wallace Dougall of San Francisco, who purchased foundation stock in 1920 from Barron and Orr. In the 1920s Goodspeed's Kennels, Harry Carney and D. W. Dawson were also located in Iowa, and in South Dakota, J. L. Schmidt and Charles Morgan. Among Canadian breeders who advertised was Harry Felt of Findlater of Saskatchewan. On the East Coast the Hurst family who had linebred Chesapeakes for more than fifty years, known as the ''Lego's Point'' strain, established Chesacroft Kennels at Lutherville, Maryland. The Chesacroft kennel name was carried on in the 1930s by Anthony A. Bliss, who became president of the American Chesapeake Club in 1934 and moved the club's headquarters to the East. Enthusiastic and innovative, he stimulated great activity among Chesapeake owners and many new kennels were started:

- **Native Shore** kennels, belonging to Mrs. Royce R. Spring, near Easton, Maryland.
- **Dilwyne**, from the name of Robert Carpenter's place in Montchanin, Delaware.
- **Marvadel** kennels, belonging to J. Gould Remick, who had both Labradors and Chesapeakes, and also ran Curly-Coated Retrievers successfully in Field Trials, near Easton, Maryland.
- **Chesdel** kennels, started in 1935 by M. Alexander Spear, near Dover, Delaware.
- **Cocoa King** kennels was established by Ferdinand A. Bunte, at his Springcrest Farm, Genoa City, Wisconsin, as the legacy of Cocoa King, one of Mr. Bunte's first outstanding Chesapeake dogs.
- **Ducklore** was the name of Arthur Storz's hunting lodge in Nebraska, where his kennel also specialized in producing a super hunting strain.

  Mr. Storz and Mr. Bunte both followed the ducks from the early fall opening of the Canadian season through the American season, and later down on into Mexico—almost half a year of hunting, and their Chesapeakes made this pilgrimage with them.
- **Grizzley Island** kennels, belonging to Louis Traung, was on the Suisun marshes near San Francisco. Mr. Traung purchased a great many dogs, among them Ch. Chesacroft Nippy Bob, and bred extensively for bench and field. Even today, in Northern California, his bloodlines are in most of the shooting dog pedigrees.

Ch. Bud Parker's Ripple, Best of Breed, ACC Specialty Show 1933. Owned by Anthony A. Bliss, she had a great record on the bench, was seldom if ever defeated and was the first Chesapeake bitch to place in the Sporting Group.

Ch. The Second Cocoa, owned by Ferdinand Bunte, one of the best-known dogs of his era. He participated in Field Trials, won consistently on the bench and was a superb hunting dog.

FORM AND FUNCTION

In the decade from 1930 to 1940, forty bench championships were made. Eight were owned by Anthony Bliss, who had in 1932 purchased the Chesacroft Kennels and relocated to his residence on Long Island. Five champions belonged to R. R. M. Carpenter, four to Philip Dater, whose **Napeague** kennels were on Long Island, and two each to Mrs. Spring and to C. W. Berg, who owned **Lake Como** kennels in Delaware.

Obedience was officially recognized by the American Kennel Club in 1936. Unofficial tests were held with all-breed shows in 1934 and 1935, and at Somerset Hills in a Novice class of twelve entries, Bud Parker Bang, a Chesapeake owned by J. Gould Remick, was one of three to qualify, placing third with 81 out of a possible 100 points. Bang was an eager and hard-going competitor in Field Trials. The first two Chesapeakes to attain the Companion Dog title were Bay Bum (in 1937) owned by Allein W. Owens, Jr., and Daybreak (in 1938) owned by Mrs. Owens.

The first AKC licensed Field Trial for retrievers in this country was put on by the Labrador Club on December 31, 1931—for Labradors only. The American Chesapeake Club put on its first trial November 27, 1932, a Specialty Trial—for Chesapeakes only. The club continued the event every year until 1941, when war interfered. Chesapeakes more than held their own in competition with Labradors, Curly-Coated Retrievers and Irish Water Spaniels in the early retriever trials.

The decade from 1940 to 1950 started well, but then the war came along and shut down many breeding programs. However, several new kennels sprang up. In the Midwest, **Mount Joy** kennels was owned by Robert and Jessie Brown of Davenport, Iowa. At first they produced show dogs, but in the 1950s Bob became interested in Field Trials and had Charles Morgan train Field Ch. and Amateur Field Ch. Nelgard's King Tut. Bob Brown died in the late 1950s, and in 1960 the Mount Joy name was acquired from his estate by Helen and Ed Fleischmann. Both the Fleischmanns are now dead and the Mount Joy name is inactive.

Wisconong kennels was registered in 1947 by William Hoard of Fort Atkinson, Wisconsin; it is a combination of two Indian names—Wisconsin and Koshkonong, the big lake where Bill often hunted. His first Chesapeake was bought to work in freezing waters, in 1946. Being pleased with this dog, he bought Deerwood Trigger from Phil Gagnon and had him trained by Charles Morgan. Trigger made both Amateur and Open Field Trial champion, and produced excellent shooting dogs, among them Ch. Wisconong Jodri, owned and trained by Mrs. W. H. Drisko;

Ch. Wisconong Jodri, UDT, taking the high jump for her owner and trainer, Mrs. W. H. Drisko of Wayzata, Minnesota. Jodri was the first Chesapeake Utility Dog.

this was the first Chesapeake to make the Utility Dog title. Being equally successful in Tracking, Jodri became the first Chesapeake UDT. Wisconong Kennels disappeared with Mr. Hoard's death.

Deerwood was the kennel name of Philip Gagnon of Minnesota, who bred some outstanding dogs, and personally trained his bitch, Field Ch. and Amateur Field Ch. Raindrop of Deerwood, who was an exceptional performer. Deerwood has been inactive since Mr. Gagnon died. **Kamiakin** was one of the first northwestern kennel names, used by D. R. Irons of Seattle, Washington. He bred and showed Parker's Airline Peggy to her bench championship. In the late 1940s, Russ Irons became active in West Coast Field Trials, and one of the best Field Trial dogs "of any breed," to quote Eloise Cherry, was Duke of Kamiakin. The Kamiakin name was abandoned when Mr. Irons died.

Fifty-three bench championships were made from 1940 to 1950, forty-five of them by eastern dogs. As a result of the war, especially in the East, it was 1948 before the shows got back to normal. The leading exhibitors in this period were Mrs. Royce Spring, Mrs. Allein Owens, Jr., Dr. Helen Ingleby and Eugene V. Weems in the East, Mount Joy Kennels and Ferdinand Bunte in the Midwest and D. R. Irons and Louis Traung in the West.

There were few obedience exhibitors in these years. Seventeen Chesapeakes earned the Companion Dog title, and three the Companion Dog Excellent. The majority of owners lived in the East. Eloise Heller attracted much attention showing her Grizzley Bear to his CD in San Francisco because many people believed this breed to be too tough to be handled by a woman.

Field Trials also were hard hit by the war and postwar years. Younger men went into the armed services, breeding was curtailed and some kennels were broken up during those years; travel was restricted because of gas rationing. On Long Island there were enough qualified dogs to continue holding at least a few licensed trials, but in Delaware, where Chesapeake interest was strong, in most cases only sanctioned trials could be held. Certainly there were dogs deserving of Field Championships that were denied by these circumstances the opportunity to make the title. Five Field Championships were attained with Chesapeakes: E. K. Ward with Sodak Rip, E. Monroe Osborne with Guess of Shagwong, R. N. Crawford with Chesacroft Baron, Vance Morris and his Bayle and Dr. George Gardner with the great bitch Tiger of Clipper City. All of these competed in the National Retriever Championship Stakes, which started in 1942.

Despite the lack of formal activity in this period, American Kennel Club registrations increased each year. In 1938, there were only 178 individual Chesapeake registrations. By 1945, the total had risen to 427, and in 1950 there were 543.

There was, and always will be, a loyal and dedicated group of Chesapeake owners. Without a doubt, the Chesapeake is an all-around dog, and their owners feel that this breed possesses many qualities not easily found in other breeds. For many of us, there is no other dog.

2

The Modern Chesapeake Bay Retriever

"TIME DIMINISHES the importance of both breeders and bloodlines, especially if the bloodlines have not been kept up and there are no direct descendants that can be used for breeding today." When, in 1951, William Hoard, Jr., became the president of the American Chesapeake Club, his boundless energy and skillful leadership resulted in a great stimulus for the breed.

This was the observation made by Eloise Heller Cherry who dated her familiarity with the breed from about that time. Having begun to hunt over her first Chesapeakes, Eloise also began to show a few Chesapeakes on the bench, compete with them in Obedience and bring some pups to the early West Coast Field Trials. She remarked that she traveled a great deal and so was able to see bench shows and Field Trials in many different areas, and to become acquainted with quite a few exhibitors of that time. I was one with whom acquaintance ripened into friendship. I must add that Eloise's enthusiasm, warm, outgoing personality and talent for leadership all combined to provide a stimulus equal to that generated by Bill Hoard. We in Chesapeakes were fortunate in our leaders in those days.

For our purposes here, we will list early kennels and breeders whose contributions in all disciplines—conformation, Field and Obedience—became a secure foundation for present-day success in the breed, as well as for all that is yet to follow.

Ch. Eastern Waters' Baronessa, TD. Best of Breed in three successive ACC Specialty Shows, 1964, 1965, 1966. Bred, owned and handled by Janet Horn. 'Nessa's Specialty record began with Winners Bitch from Puppy Class 1962, and Best of Opposite Sex in 1963. Her wins included 48 Bests of Breed, among them Westminster 1963, and a Sporting Group III.

Eastern Waters	Janet and Dr. Daniel Horn
Chesachobee	Mildred Buchholz
Chesdel	Alex Spear
Chesarab	Sheila and Richard DiVaccaro
West River	Eugene Weems
Chessy	Ralph Mock
Alpine	Fred Woodall
Chesanoma/Mount Joy	Mr./Mrs. E. C. Fleischmann
Heller	Eloise and Walter Heller
Tengri	Eugene and Mary Pantzer
Aleutian	Dr. John Lundy
Longcove	The Kinney Family
Koolwaters	The Kreuger Family
Burning Tree	Dr. Marston and Judy Jones
Chestnut Hill	The Anderson Family
Cherokee	The Urban Family
Cur-San	Curt and Sandy Dollar
Rigbys	Clyde and Jack Rigby
Crosswinds	Kent and Fran Lowman

FC/AFC Atom Bob, bred, owned, trained and handled by Dr. John Lundy.

Chesapine	Ray and Lorraine Berg
Chesareid	William and Sybil Reid
Von Nassau	A. Mesdag
Hi-Ho	Stephen and Ellen Loftsgaard
Dunnell's Ranch	Adey May Dunnell
Snocree	Dr. and Mrs. John Schmidt
Baronland	Eloise Heller
Larson's	Lyle Larson
Native Shore	Mrs. Royce Spring/(later) Alice and Walter Hansen
Chesrite	Jan and Jody Thomas
Northcreek	The Hoagland Family
Oak 'n' Thistle	Drs. James and Brenda Stewart
Blustrywood	Karen and John Wood, Jr.
Berteleda	Nancy and Les Lowenthal
Wyndham	Edward Atkins, Jr.
Redlion	Jane Pappler

As we move into the 1980s, we see many new kennels on the scene, with interest in the versatility of the Chesapeake remaining strong.

The **Pond Hollow** kennels of Dyane and Bill Baldwin of Newport, Pennsylvania, had their first litter in 1979, with co-breeder Barbara Mullen, which produced Ch. Mitsu Kuma's Swamp Scout, CD, WD, and Ch. Mitsu Kuma's Pond Mist, CD, JH, WD, who along with Ch. Mitsu Kuma's Saxon Pond, UD, WD, formed the basis of the Pond Hollow breeding stock. This name was first used in 1981, derived from the local term for little valleys or hollows among the hills. The Baldwins have personally trained and handled their dogs in conformation, Obedience and hunting tests, and have always felt that Chesapeakes should be all-around dogs. They consider their most notable dogs to be Ch. Pond Hollow Excalibur, CD, WD, Ch. Pond Hollow Spindrift, CD, SH, WDX, and Ch. Pond Hollow Wild Goose Chase.

Jon and Carol Andersen started **Caroway** kennels in Lake Forest, Illinois, and became prominent in the 1980s with their success in Field Trials and a breeding program that produced several dual champions. **Sunshine** kennels was established by Steve and Sharon Parker to breed Field Trial and hunting dogs at McCammon, Idaho, following their spectacular success in Field Trials with FC/AFC Elijah's Sunshine Sally and her offspring. In southern California, Arthur and Mary Ellen Mazzola began their **Z's** kennels, producing bench champions and running dogs in Field Trials. Mary Ellen says she chose "Z" because it would always be at the end of alphabetical listings, since the beginnings are preempted by many names beginning with "A." She got her first Chesapeake in 1969, and has always tried for the all-round dog, "good in field, show, Obedience and number one in home life." The **Sandy Oaks** kennel was started in 1973 by Dave and Kathy Miller with one Chesapeake and several Lhasas at Sebastopol, California. Ch. Baron's Sandy Bay, CD, WD, aroused Kathy's interest in the breed almost to the point of obsession, and while carrying on a limited breeding program she has striven to learn everything she could about the Chesapeake, past and present. Sandy Oaks dogs are shown in conformation and Obedience and worked in the field, linebred on leading Field Trial champions, dual champions, and they are producing field, show and Obedience dogs, and "just plain, hardworking, lovable pets!" Kathy's all-time favorite was Ch. Sandy's Hi-Ho Shooting Star, UD, JH, WDX, CGC.

In 1982 **Port Side** was adopted by Ron and Ginny Reed of New Cumberland, Pennsylvania; this is a family who train and show their Chesapeakes in conformation, Obedience and field. The Reeds' young daughters have been active in Junior Showmanship, and their parents

16

Ch. Berteleda Maggie, UD, WDX, and Ch. Cub's Marin Echo, UD, WD, two handsome specimens owned by Les and Nancy Lowenthal, and trained by Nancy. They also served as Les's hunting dogs.

Ch. Wyndham's Algonquin, TDX, WD. Ch. Windown Aelwif of Wyndham. Wyndham's Arapahoe. Ch. Canadian Cub of Wyndham. Ch. Windown Bull of Bull Hill. Here is represented the foundation Chesapeake breeding of Ed Atkins's Wyndham Kennels.

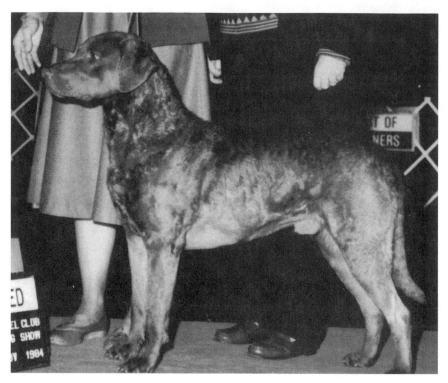

Ch. Pond Hollow Excalibur, CD, WD, winning Best of Breed in the once-in-a-lifetime American Kennel Club Centennial Dog Show. Judge: Hayden Martin. Breeder-Handler: Dyane Baldwin. Owner: Kathryn Longer. "Callie" was a consistent breed winner and had several Sporting Group placements.

have been especially active in hunting tests. **Fitzhugh** kennels came into being with Madelyn Conner's purchase of a bitch for breeding, Shannon of Fitzhugh. Bred to Am. & Can. Ch. Eastern Waters' Chargn Knight, CD, Shannon produced the Conners' first show dog Ch. Jacob of Fitz-hugh, CD, WD. Eastern Waters' Fitzhugh Cuan was bred to Jake to produce the great contender Ch. Fitzhugh's Bag The Limit, CD, WDX. Fitzhugh is the name of a small creek on the Conner property in Maryland. Meghan Conner joined forces with Darren Sausser who had inaugurated the name **Shorvue** and they moved the Fitzhugh Kennels to Smyrna, Delaware, to carry on a small, conscientious program based on Eastern Waters lines. True students of the breed, they are proud of their dogs' soundness, structurally and mentally, and versatility plays an important part in their breeding plans.

In Michigan, Jim and Carole Bomberger established their **Parklake** kennels, having started with a hunting dog in 1978. Their first litter

Ch. Jacob, Duke of Fitzhugh, CD, WD. Bred and owned by Madelyn Conner. "Jake," a Sporting Group winner, was a son of Best in Show Ch. Eastern Waters' Chargn Knight, CD. Jake sired Best in Show Ch. Fitzhugh's Bag the Limit, CD, WDX, making three generations of Group I winners.

produced five champions, enthusiastically shown by the Bombergers themselves and their family members, and at the end of the decade they have produced about twenty champions. **Wild Mountain** Chesapeakes, owned by Mark Kaufman and Linda Allington, started in 1980 at West Brookfield, Massachusetts, with their foundation sire, Ch. Poisett's Starboarder Morgan, CD, MH, WDQ. Their foundation bitch, Chesrite's Wild Mountain Tyme, CD, WDQ, inspired their kennel name. Their primary focus is field work, but their dogs also enjoy showing in breed and Obedience rings, and in Agility. **Homespun** Chesapeakes in Telford, Pennsylvania, was established by Marie Guthier in 1982, and is best known for all-around dogs, having produced bench champions, titled hunting dogs, Delta Society and therapy dogs, search and rescue and Obedience dogs. Marie is most proud of littermates Ch. Homespun's Ruffled Feathers, a National Specialty show judge's Award of Merit at age fourteen months, and her brother Ch. Homespun's Snooker, a multiple Group placer.

Meadowood is the kennel name of Sylvia Holderman of Santa Cruz, California, and it is found on champion- and Obedience-titled dogs and several with hunting test titles. **Snowfield** kennels is owned by Kellie Lewis and Lone Nielsen, located in Somerset, California. Their foundation bitch was Ch. Stoneycreek Hopscotch, CD; bred only once, she produced three champions, and her son Ch. Snowfields Double Scotch, CD, WD, has many Bests of Breed and a Group I to his credit. **Sea-Moors** is the prefix used by Kevin and Rosemary Seymour of Wolcott, New York, who show their Chesapeakes in conformation, and are very active in field work, especially hunting tests with both NAHRA and AKC tests available. **Chesabar** kennels in Bridgeton, New Jersey, was founded by Patsy and Rudy Barber and began to breed winning Chesapeakes for show, Obedience, hunting and family companionship in 1983, proving that good-looking dogs can also be bred to behave and hunt. Their breeding program stems from their first Chesapeake, Shorewaters Bussy, through his sons Am. & Can. Ch. Baron of Shorewaters Bussy and Ch. Ashby of Shorewaters Bussy, CD, WD, JH.

Rocky Creek retrievers was established in 1974 by Geraldine Mines and her daughters Janice Bykowsky, Kathy Rayner and Sharon Mines. Geraldine and Sharon continue to breed and show Labradors; Janice and her son breed and show Labradors and Chesapeakes since Janice and Kathy acquired their first Chesapeake in 1982, their foundation bitch, Am. & Can. Ch. Snocree's Golden Beast of RC, CD, CGC, who won her Companion Dog title at the age of ten, after an impressive career as a specials bitch and a top producer. **Nativeland** is the kennel name adopted by Rich and Rachel Young, after they had bred several litters from foundation stock Ch. Homespun's Young Gator, JH, and Ch. Chestnut Hill's Sienna Sage. They emphasize field work as they continue to show in conformation. They are located in East Greenville, Pennsylvania. **Nuka Bay** is the prefix chosen by Lynda Barber of Anchorage, Alaska. Lynda has made a fine record in Obedience with her Chesapeakes as well as showing several to their championships. **Chalktaw** kennels owned by Lindsey and Tom Chalkley was established in 1985 in Canyon Lake, Texas. Their whole family, including two children Evaleen and Thomas, participates in the training and care, and Lindsey writes that Chalktaw dogs are proving their versatility in a very competitive world.

Field Trial interest flourished in the 1980s and seven Chesapeakes made *both* Field Championships and Amateur Field Championships. Including these among Field Champions, a total of eleven Chesapeakes attained the FC title, and eleven AFCs were also awarded in this period.

"Tok" and "Kobuk" pulling Lynda Barber across the finish line in the Anchorage Fur Rendezvous Skijoring Race. These are littermates bred by Lynda and trained and handled by her to Championship and Obedience titles in both the United States and Canada.

Four Field Champions competed in the shows to become dual champions, bringing the all-time total for the breed to eleven.

In conformation shows, 872 Champions finished in the decade from 1980 to 1989, and 275 championships were earned from 1990 through 1992, giving a total of 1,147 in the twelve-year period. More Chesapeakes were shown in this period than ever before. In Obedience, 736 Companion Dog titles were earned from 1980 through 1992, bringing the all-time total of Chesapeake CDs to 1,260.

This evidence of consistent participation in AKC competitive events shows a healthy growth and progress made by the breed, for which the American Kennel Club registered 5,295 Chesapeakes in 1992. We continue to move forward.

SKULL broad, round

EYES medium large, wide apart, yellowish or amber

STOP medium

LIPS thin, not pendulous

MUZZLE pointed but not sharp; teeth not undershot or overshot

CHEST strong, deep, wide; barrel round

LEGS medium length, straight, good bone, muscular, very powerful; dewclaws may be removed on forelegs, must be removed on hindlegs

COAT thick, short, not over 1½" long; oily; undercoat dense, fine wooly; outercoat harsh, water-resistant (as a duck's feathers); hair on legs, face, should be short, straight

COLOR: Dark brown to faded tan or any shade of deadgrass; white spot (smaller the better) on breast, toes and belly permissible; solid and self-colored dogs preferred.

EARS small, set high, hanging loose, medium-thick leather

NECK medium-length, strong, muscular, tapering

SHOULDERS sloping; full liberty of action with plenty power, unrestricted movement

BACK short, well-coupled, powerful

PASTERNS medium length, slightly bent

FLANKS well tucked up

APPEARANCE: Well-proportioned, well-balanced, general outline impressive; body length medium; not cobby, not roached; coat texture and color an essential consideration.

SIZE: Weight—males 65-80 lbs.
bitches 55-70 lbs.
Height - males 23-26"
bitches 21-24"

Oversized or undersized dogs to be severely penalized

TAIL medium heavy at base; moderate feathering permissible, but over 1¾" long a disqualification; not to curl over back or side kink

HINDQUARTERS trifle higher than shoulders, especially powerful to supply swimming power

HOCK to HEEL not too long or too short

FEET hare, well-webbed, good size; toes well-rounded and close

DISQUALIFICATIONS: Black colored. Dewclaws on hind legs; white on any part of body except breast, belly, or spots on feet; feathering on tail or legs over 1¾" long; undershot, overshot, or any deformity; coat curly or tendency to curl all over body; specimens unworthy or lacking in breed characteristics.

22

3

Standard for the Chesapeake Bay Retriever

GENERAL APPEARANCE

Equally proficient on land and in the water, the Chesapeake Bay Retriever was developed along the Chesapeake Bay to hunt waterfowl under the most adverse weather and water conditions, often having to break ice during the course of many strenuous multiple retrieves. Frequently the Chesapeake must face wind, tide and long cold swims in its work. The breed's characteristics are specifically suited to enable the Chesapeake to function with ease, efficiency and endurance. In head, the Chesapeake's skull is broad and round with a medium stop. The jaws should be of sufficient length and strength to carry large game birds with an easy, tender hold. The double coat consists of a short, harsh, wavy outer coat and a dense, fine, wooly undercoat containing an abundance of natural oil, and is ideally suited for the icy rugged conditions of weather the Chesapeake often works in. In body, the Chesapeake is a strong, well-balanced, powerfully built animal of moderate size and medium length in body and leg, deep and wide in chest, the shoulders built with full liberty of movement and with no tendency to weakness in any feature, particularly the rear. The power, though, should not be at the expense of agility or stamina. Size and substance should not be excessive, as this is a working retriever of an active nature.

Distinctive features include eyes that are very clear, of yellowish or amber hue, hindquarters as high or a trifle higher than the shoulders and a double coat which tends to wave on shoulders, neck, back and loins only.

The Chesapeake is valued for its bright and happy disposition, intelligence, quiet good sense and affectionate, protective nature. Extreme shyness or extreme aggressive tendencies are not desirable in the breed either as a gun dog or companion.

Disqualifications: Specimens that are lacking in breed characteristics should be disqualified.

SIZE, PROPORTION, SUBSTANCE

HEIGHT: Males should measure twenty-three to twenty-six inches; females should measure twenty-one to twenty-four inches. *Oversized* or *undersized* animals *are* to be *severely penalized.*

PROPORTION: Height from the top of the shoulder blades to the ground should be slightly less than the body length from the breastbone to the point of buttocks. Depth of body should extend at least to the elbow. Shoulder to elbow and elbow to ground should be equal.

WEIGHT: Males should weigh sixty-five to eighty pounds; females should weigh fifty-five to seventy pounds.

HEAD: The Chesapeake Bay Retriever should have an intelligent expression. *Eyes* are to be medium large, very clear, of yellowish or amber color and wide apart. *Ears* are to be small, set well up on the head, hanging loosely and of medium leather. *Skull* is broad and round with a medium stop. *Nose* is medium short. *Muzzle* is approximately the same length as the skull, tapered, pointed but not sharp. *Lips* are thin, not pendulous.

BITE: Scissors is preferred, but a level bite is acceptable.

Disqualifications: Either undershot or overshot bites are to be disqualified.

NECK, TOPLINE, BODY: *Neck* should be of medium length with a strong muscular appearance, tapering to the shoulders. *Topline* should show the hindquarters to be as high as or a trifle higher than the shoulders. *Back* should be short, well coupled and powerful. *Chest* should be strong, deep and wide, rib cage barrel round and deep. *Body* is of medium length, neither cobby nor roached, but rather approaching hollowness from underneath as the flanks should be well tucked up. *Tail* of medium length; medium heavy at the base. The tail should be straight or slightly curved and should not curl over back or side kink.

FOREQUARTERS: There should be no tendency to weakness in the forequarters. *Shoulders* should be sloping with full liberty of action, plenty of power and without any restrictions of movement. *Legs* should be medium in length and straight, showing good bone and muscle, pasterns slightly bent and of medium length. The front legs should appear straight when viewed from front or rear. Dewclaws on the forelegs may be removed. Well-webbed hare feet should be of good size with toes well rounded and close.

HINDQUARTERS: Good hindquarters are essential. They should show fully as much power as the forequarters. There should be no tendency to weakness in the hindquarters. Hindquarters should be especially powerful to supply the driving power for swimming. Legs should be medium length and straight, showing good bone and muscle. Stifles should be well angulated. The distance from hock to ground should be of medium length. The hind legs should look straight when viewed from the front or rear. Dewclaws, if any, must be removed from the hind legs.

Disqualifications: Dewclaws on the hind legs are a disqualification.

COAT: Coat should be thick and short, nowhere over 1½ inches long, with a dense fine wooly undercoat. Hair on the face and legs should be very short and straight with a tendency to wave on the shoulders, neck, back and loins only. Moderate feathering on rear of hindquarters and tail is permissible.

The texture of the Chesapeake's coat is very important, as the Chesapeake is used for hunting under all sorts of adverse weather conditions, often working in ice and snow. The oil in the harsh outer coat and wooly undercoat is of extreme value in preventing the cold water from reaching the Chesapeake's skin and aids in quick drying. A Chesapeake's coat should resist the water in the same way that a duck's feathers do. When the Chesapeake leaves the water and shakes, the coat should not hold water at all, being merely moist.

Disqualifications: A coat that is curly or has a tendency to curl all over the body must be disqualified. Feathering on the tail or legs over 1¾ inches long must be disqualified.

COLOR: The color of the Chesapeake Bay Retriever must be nearly that of its working surroundings as possible. Any color of brown, sedge or deadgrass is acceptable, self-colored Chesapeakes being preferred. One color is not to be preferred over another. A white spot on the breast, belly, toes or back of the feet (immediately above the large pad) is permissible, but the smaller the spot, the better, solid colored preferred. The color of the coat and its texture must be given every consideration when judging on the bench or in the ring. Honorable scars are not to be penalized.

Disqualifications: Black colored, white on any part of the body except breast, belly, toes or back of feet must be disqualified.

GAIT: The gait should be smooth, free and effortless, giving the impression of great power and strength. When viewed from the side, there should be good reach with no restrictions of movement in the front and plenty of drive in the rear, with good flexion of the stifle and hock joints. Coming at you, there should be no sign of elbows being out. When the Chesapeake is moving away from you, there should be no sign of cow-hockness from the rear. As speed increases, the feet tend to converge toward a center line of gravity.

TEMPERAMENT: The Chesapeake Bay Retriever should show a bright and happy disposition with an intelligent expression. Courage, willingness to work, alertness, nose, intelligence, love of water, general quality and, most of all, disposition should be given primary consideration in the selection and breeding of the Chesapeake Bay Retriever.

DISQUALIFICATIONS

1. Specimens lacking in breed characteristics.
2. Teeth overshot or undershot.
3. Dewclaws on the hind legs.
4. Coat curly or with a tendency to curl all over the body.

5. Feathering on the tail or legs over 1¾ inches long.
6. Black colored.
7. White on any part of the body except breast, belly, toes, or back of feet.

The question of coat and general type of balance takes precedence over any scoring table which could be drawn up. The Chesapeake should be well proportioned, an animal with a good coat and well balanced in other points being preferable to one excelling in some but weak in others.

POSITIVE SCALE OF POINTS

Head, including lips, ears and eyes 16
Neck 4
Shoulders and body. 12
Hindquarters and stifles 12
Elbows, legs and feet 12
Color 4
Stern and tail 10
Coat and texture 18
General conformation 12
Total 100

APPROXIMATE MEASUREMENTS

INCHES

Length head, nose to occiput . . . . 9½ to 10
Girth at ears . . . . 20 to 21
Muzzle below eyes . . . . 10 to 10½
Length of ears . . . . 4½ to 5
Width between eyes . . . . 2½ to 2¾
Girth neck close to shoulder . . . . 20 to 22
Girth at flank . . . . 24 to 25
Length from occiput to tail base . . . . 34 to 35
Girth forearms at shoulders . . . . 10 to 10½
Girth upper thigh . . . . 19 to 20
From root to root of ear, over skull . . . . 5 to 6
Occiput to top shoulder blades . . . . 9 to 9½
From elbow to elbow over the shoulders . . . . 25 to 26

Approved: November 9, 1993
Effective: December 31, 1993

Chesapeake swimming style demonstrated by Maya Mächler's "Water-Lovers." Note toplines just below water level, high hindquarters, and tails as straight, level extensions of the backline. There is no wasted motion, and little water resistance in their speed and efficiency. Each dog leaves a wake like a canoe.

4

Commentary on the Chesapeake Standard

THE FIRST SECTION of this version of the breed Standard is a new one, written to meet the American Kennel Club requirement that a breed Standard should begin with a general description of the breed and its original purpose. As I read this section, the work of the breed is in every case related to type features, and there is little that I might add.

The yellowish eye has always been a type characteristic of this breed, varying darker or lighter to blend with the color of the coat. The high hindquarters are to be explained in the words of an old-time trainer who told me, "the Chesapeake is the greatest water-dog there ever was *because* he carries his rear high in the water." Hindquarters as high as or higher than the shoulders are a requirement for efficiency and power in swimming, and are not to be associated with a soft or swayback, for a strong back is important to carry the thrust of the powerful hindquarters forward to the equally powerful front assembly. This breed must have great flexibility for maneuverability in water as well as on land, and the topline may appear level or it may show a visible rise behind.

Although the coat is asked to wave on shoulders, back and loins only, a true double coat must well cover the flanks and sides where the wave tapers gently to the short, but no less thick, almost furlike hair that protects the lower body and legs. A truly great coat is often characterized by a tufted appearance, as the thickness of the hair causes it to stand off instead of lying flat.

Breed character is well expressed, as is the breed's true nature.

SIZE

Although the severe penalty for oversize or undersize is applied only to height, weight in relation to height should be taken into account. The dog that is overboned, coarse, cloddy and whose proportions suggest a large Working breed rather than an active, agile Sporting dog should be severely penalized even though height may not exceed the Standard specifications.

HEAD

On head, ears are set high because this is a swimming dog, and low-set ears will ship more water. In reading "broad and round," we refer back to the table of measurements at the end of the Standard, where we find distance from root to root of ear to be five to six inches—not, please, ten to twelve inches. We are *not to construe this as meaning the broader the better*. The proportions of the head given here are drawn from these measurements.

I do not know why one sees so many loose, thick pendulous lips and the appearance of a squared-off muzzle in this breed, when the Standard is so clear on this and on a tapering, slightly pointed muzzle.

BODY

In general the description of body and running gear needs no comment. One might point out that a wide chest must not be so wide as to interfere with the action of the forequarters, which are to have full liberty of action, and should show enough length of upper arm to *prevent* restricted front movement.

The hare foot, well webbed, functions best in swimming water, in mud and soggy marshes and in snow and ice. In field work on land this foot gives greater speed to the running dog.

COAT AND COLOR

Although the format for this Standard provides for the separation of coat and color, in actuality they cannot be separated, for the texture of the coat and the color are both determined by the amount and distribution of pigment. The deadgrass color includes any shade of deadgrass, varying from a tan to a dull straw color. In considering tan, one discovers that there are also in existence a wide range of hues of tan. Deadgrass is particularly characterized by the variation of intensity of pigment and shades of the basic color producing the camouflage effect that blends a dog with the working surroundings, and the varying shades of deadgrass will as often as not be found on the same dog.

GAIT

The section on gait is a new one as requested by the American Kennel Club. Obviously the dog should move with the soundness, reach and drive of any good Sporting dog. To look further, this is a swimming dog with legs that carry the dog through water as well as on land.

What we can see in the dog's movement on land is what the legs are doing in the water. The sloping shoulder with plenty of power with full liberty of action is essential for efficiency in swimming, and as feet converge with increased speed, they cut through the water and reduce resistance. All the requirements for correct gait on land are essential for the best performance in the water.

TEMPERAMENT

It has always been my thought that the Standard is intended as a guide to breeders as well as judges, so I have not worried much about a judge's problems in evaluating some of these qualities in the ring. It is up to the breeders not to overlook the qualities the dog shows at home and in the field even though they cannot be assessed in the ring. We can make the judge's task more enjoyable by presenting our dogs so as to show as many of these positive qualities as possible. Sometimes a little training and familiarization with ring conditions is all that is needed to bring out the dog's willingness to work in that environment, for not all work is retrieving game; *work can be anything the owner asks the dog to do.*

DISQUALIFICATIONS

The seven disqualifications in our Standard were first laid down in 1936, and at that time, I was told by one who had worked on the Standard Committee in the 1930s, these items were made disqualifications because they were serious problems in the breed. If they are now found only infrequently it is a tribute to the emphasis implied by the potential for disqualification. We need to retain these disqualifications, for anything that has previously been a problem in the breed can become one again if we do not keep alert and guard against it.

SCALE OF POINTS AND APPROXIMATE MEASUREMENTS

The "Scale of Points" and the "Approximate Measurements" are outside the AKC format; however, they have been part of the Chesapeake Bay Retriever Standard for thirty years, and so it was the belief of our committee that they should be retained. Perhaps it is something about the mentality of Chesapeake people, for the first attempt at laying down a Standard for the breed in 1877 specified desired weights and measurements. Many of us feel that these tables express proportions in a way that helps us to understand them. As novices, many of us also found them useful in the evaluation of our own dogs.

It is clear that coat is the single most important type feature of the breed. Yet many times Chesapeakes are shown out of coat or with coats that could never meet the Standard description.

It is not a "head breed." However, with head only slightly less than coat in importance as a single feature, more attention should be paid to the Standard's requirements for the head than appears to be the case. We do want the sound and balanced dog implied by the total points for shoulders and body, hindquarters and stifles, elbows, legs and feet, and the importance of a well-formed, properly carried tail cannot be ignored for it can detract from the general conformation, or it can enhance it. The statement that an animal with a good coat and well balanced in other points is preferable to one excelling in some but weak in others often leads to a reward for mediocrity, when the question of coat is satisfied by a dog more or less covered with some kind of hair. We must look for a good coat, and *then* evaluate the animal.

The function of the measurements is to convey an idea of size and of proportion. They are approximate, and no dog is expected to meet them with mathematical exactitude; however, gross deviation implies a deviation from correct type.

Responding to the AKC's request to fit our Standard into their prescribed format, the Standard Committee consisting of Chairperson Lorraine Berg in Wisconsin, Dyane Baldwin in Pennsylvania, Sally Diess in Oregon, Brenda Stewart in Maryland and Janet Horn in New Jersey defined its aims and spent nearly four years in voluminous correspondence, seeking opinions and suggestions from approved judges and from fanciers, and delving exhaustively into every point that seemed to be at issue.

We were aware that sections in our current Standard were so expressed as to generate confusion and misconceptions in judges and breeders alike, and it was our objective to identify, explain and clarify these confusing sections. In the course of changing wording to effect these clarifications, and changing and adding newly worded sections as required by the AKC, our third consideration was to do these things in such a way as not to make any changes in the basic requirements of the Standard as it had stood with little alteration for over fifty years, and certainly to do our best to avoid making any changes that might change the breed.

All of us have bred and shown Chesapeakes, trained and handled them in Obedience and in the field; some of us have had experience in Tracking, and we all share our homes with Chesapeakes as family dogs and hunting companions. It has been an honor and a privilege to serve on this committee.

Dr. Daniel Horn awarding BOB to Ch. Longcove's Spring Serenade, CD, WD, owned by Jeannie and Kathy Kinney, shown here by Kathy.

5

Judging the Chesapeake Bay Retriever

THE CHESAPEAKE COAT
BY DR. DANIEL HORN

Coat has been the most important type feature in the description of the Chesapeake Bay Retriever, predating the earliest attempts to prepare a written Standard. Yet in the endless evaluating of Chesapeakes that goes on among owners, breeders, would-be breeders and judges, coat has become the most misunderstood and ignored characteristic of the breed. This despite the explanatory note in the Standard that "the question of coat and general type of balance takes precedence over any scoring table which could be drawn up."

If a Chesapeake's coat looks like that of a Golden, Labrador or other retriever breed, it is an improper coat; if it looks like that of an Irish Water Spaniel or a Rhodesian Ridgeback or a Newfoundland or a German Shorthaired Pointer it is a bad coat. *Type characteristics are what distinguish one breed from another, and if we ignore these we might just as well be evaluating mongrels.* The coat of a Chesapeake should be unlike the coat of any other breed.

Since the Chesapeake coat is unique, it requires a complex description. A good Chesapeake coat has a springy, bouncy feeling, not only along the topline, but well down the flanks, and the dog is well covered all over. This springiness comes from the thick, soft wooly undercoat that imparts a wave or a crinkled tufted appearance to the harsher outer coat; the hairs curve but do not form ringlets.

The Chesapeake coat, however, does *not* consist of two sets of hairs, one soft and the other harsh, but comes from differences in texture that depend on the way the pigment is distributed along the hair. The part of the individual hair that is close to the hair follicle has little pigment, and what there is has a very even distribution without clumping of the pigment, therefore imparting the soft wooly feeling. As one moves along the same hair toward the tip there are clumps of pigment that impart the harsher feeling depending on the spacing of the clumps and the concentration of pigment. It is this clumping that contributes to the harsh, water-resistant quality of the coat and is responsible for the "deadgrass" color that is unique to the breed. The variations in brown color that appear in a field of dead grass and weeds, especially in marshes, provide a perfect camouflage whether a working Chesapeake is a light or dark deadgrass. The coloring is similar to what is called the agouti pattern in some species, and in dogs "wildcolor."

A dog who does not have this clumping and variation in pigment along the individual hairs lacks the combination of the soft wooly undercoat that keeps the dog warm when working in cold, icy water and the harsher outercoat that helps repel the water so that it is not soaked up by the coat. From discussions with old-time breeders whose experience went back to the turn of the century, the objections to "liver" were against both the color and the type of coat that usually went with the smooth, shiny dark brown color that lacked the undercoat and texture variation desired. Liver color was removed as a disqualification in the Standard approved in 1976. The Standard was changed because liver was difficult to define.

The color description was changed from "solid color" to "self-colored" to emphasize that the single pigment may vary in concentration. The type of coat that liver was meant to describe is a most serious fault because it lacks the critical type feature of the multi-textured coat. A well-coated Chesapeake in full bloom is a handsome sight. It does not come about by accident; one must breed for it.

A coat that has the texture qualities described in the Standard is usually a good color. Sometimes the variation in the amount and intensity of the brown pigment gives the appearance of stripes, and when the contrast in pigment becomes too marked it can be displeasing and uncharacteristic of the breed ideal. This contrast is most marked when dogs are out of coat. It also tends to be more characteristic of puppies before their coat matures into its adult form. If exhibitors would keep their dogs out of the show ring when dogs are out of coat, it would be easier for judges to become familiar with these important Chesapeake type features. If dogs are shown out of coat and judges award point and breed wins to dogs that are out of coat, everybody loses. If a dog is shown so out of coat that the quality of the coat cannot be assessed, it may be a kindness to the exhibitor's feelings to award points or a breed win, but it is hardly a kindness to the breed. A judge has the responsibility of knowing what a Chesapeake coat is supposed to be. Should one be judging the breed if one cannot accept this responsibility?

JUDGING THE CHESAPEAKE BAY RETRIEVER
BY WILLIAM K. BOYSON

William K. Boyson showed his Ch. Eastern Waters' Big Gunpowder to Best of Breed, ACC Specialty Show 1971. He got his first Chesapeake in 1960 for hunting and trials, and became interested in Obedience and conformation showing, putting titles on Ch. Conroy's Bird, CDX, before breeding her. He then turned to judging and is an approved AKC judge.

When judging the Chesapeake Bay Retriever, one primary fact must be kept in mind—purpose. The Chesapeake breed was developed to retrieve canvasback and redhead ducks under any and all conditions. In the nineteenth century, hunters began shooting in the fall when the great flocks arrived, and continued to shoot until they left in the spring. The Chesapeake was required to retrieve one hundred or more ducks per day, in icy waters and against strong currents. When one keeps this in mind, the Standard is not difficult to understand.

When I judge a class of Chesapeakes, I look for the dog who is best equipped, both physically and mentally, to do the job. With the dog in a show pose, I take a careful look, primarily to see that the animal is set up properly. I also want to get an idea of the overall balance of the dog. I then move to the front and begin my hands-on examination.

When I first look at the head, I check expression, wanting to see a quietly confident look in eyes that are deep-set and wide apart. They should be amber in color and oval in appearance. I want a broad skull with plenty of room for brains and a muzzle with medium stop and enough depth to grasp a 2½ pound canvasback duck. I like a fairly wide nose with large nostrils able to pass plenty of air to the lungs of this dog who must swim long distances through rough water. Examining the mouth, I look for a scissor bite but will accept an even bite. I fault crooked teeth and will disqualify overshot or undershot. Bite is extremely important; the teeth hold the duck as it is carried and must not damage the bird. Ears should be well set up on the head, with leather heavy enough to allow air into the ear passage but light enough so that water pressure will clamp the ear over the canal and keep water out when the dog is diving. After the head examination, I step back and look at the chest and legs, seeking adequate depth of chest, strong bone and hare feet.

The neck I want to see is powerful and tapers from shoulders to head. Here I expect to see a slight arch and the beginning of the double coat that will be very visible further back on the body. I move my hands to the shoulders where I check the layback of the scapula, looking for an angle of 30 to 35 degrees from vertical. I cannot overemphasize the importance of proper shoulder layback. Without this, the dog cannot reach properly and has difficulty getting through the water.

I then move my hands over the shoulders feeling slope and musculature down to the chest where I check for a deep, wide barrel. This reveals an abundance of lung capacity, so necessary for a dog who must make long, difficult swims through cold, rough water. I move to the back of the dog looking for a fairly short loin, well tucked up.

As I do this I am examining coat, searching for a short, dense, wooly undercoat covered with harsh outer guard hairs. This coat combination keeps body heat in and water away from the skin. In my opinion, coat is the singular most important facet of Chesapeake Bay Retriever type. On a typical Chesapeake in full coat, it is almost impossible to get the fingers through the coat to bare skin. The coat is that dense.

Moving to the back, I'm looking for a muscular rump that is slightly higher than the withers. I expect to find the rear heavily muscled and a pelvis laid back at the same angle as the shoulder blade. Going down the hind legs I look for good angulation through the stifle joint and hock. Pasterns should be slightly bent and connect to good-sized hare feet. In back of the dog, I check topline expecting to see a back that does not sag but rises gradually, in a straight line to the rump. I expect the tail to reach near the hock with dense, heavy coat at the base, tapering to a rounded point at the tip. The ideal Chesapeake will have no feathering on the tail. The last item I check on the standing examination is the webbing in the feet. The Chesapeake uses the webs for propulsion much as a duck does.

When I examine movement, I use an L pattern. Going away from me, I look for the hind legs to drive and move closer to the centerline as the dog gains speed. I expect the hocks to be straight, neither cow-hocked nor barrel-hocked. On the horizontal leg of the L, I look for mismarking (white) on the body or anything else out of order. Coming toward me, I expect to see the front legs pulling straight toward me. I emphasize straight here; any deviation will be faulted. As the final part of the examination, I have the dog move in a circle to the end of the line. Here I can see the front legs reach and the rear legs drive. I also check topline and tail carriage. The tail should be carried slightly above horizontal while the head is held high and proud. This is the point when overall balance, or lack thereof, is best revealed.

JUDGING CHESAPEAKE BAY RETRIEVERS
BY MILDRED G. BUCHHOLZ

Mildred G. Buchholz is an internationally known judge of Chesapeake Bay Retrievers, as well as of Novice and Open Obedience and Tracking. Growing up with Chesapeakes on the Eastern Shore of Maryland, Millie started her Chesachobee Kennels in the early 1950s in Florida where she trained with the Obedience Training Club of Palm Beach County.

As each class comes into the ring, I like to walk down the line to gain an overall impression of outline, balance, type and quality before I have them gait around the ring and before individual examination.

After many years associated with this breed, it has become very near instinctive for me to glance at a dog to see if it is right or wrong.

Type is by far the most important because if a dog is not typical of the breed it is useless. I consider coat one of the most important breed characteristics. The correct coat is one with an oily, harsh, thick, dense, short, crinkled outercoat and a wooly undercoat covering the whole body, with very short hair on *face, feet* and *legs* only. It should fit the dog as a sheep pelt fits the sheep. It should protect the dog in all sorts of adverse conditions. *A dog that is out of coat should not be shown.* The color should be to camouflage them in their working environment and should include all colors from light straw to dark brown. The light sand color will have various shades. All the deadgrass colors are varied as well. Even the browns, from light to dark in color, have several shades of brown on one dog. These are the correct colors as they certainly camouflage better.

I've found that the dogs without the wooly undercoat do not have the highlights and would not camouflage them in their working environment.

I try to find the ones with the most plus points, because without these good points they are useless to further the breed's progress.

I learned a long time ago to discriminate between a good dog handled poorly and a poor dog presented very well. When a breed like the Chesapeake falls off in quality and develops a prevailing fault such as poor angulation, it is the breeders who are greatly responsible for what happened. Under these circumstances, even the best of judges cannot keep the breed on the road to improvement.

A well-proportioned Chesapeake is strong, balanced and well angulated front and rear, both when standing and gaiting. I look for free, smooth, powerful and coordinated gait. Increased speed causes feet to converge toward a center line of gravity, which is correct for Chesapeakes.

A dog with poor angulation is restricted in reach of forelegs and drive from rear legs, and has to take shorter steps and more of them. This causes a bouncing action rather than a smooth flowing action.

In judging this type of movement I can't help but think of these poor dogs struggling in their retrieves and bobbing up and down like a cork, rather than swimming correctly. If only they were put together right. After a couple of short retrieves on a fifteen pound goose, the dogs have had it.

Born and raised on the eastern shore of Maryland and having had Chesapeakes all my life, over seventy years, I feel the Standard is very well written, and when something is repeated several times, it is because that repeated feature is very important and deserves to be mentioned several times. The disqualifications in our Standard are very straightforward.

In judging Chesapeakes it is very important to find the ones with positive virtues, as they are the only ones that will further the breed's progress. It's important for judges to work with breeders to help keep our breed on the road to improvement.

Winning isn't everything—but Chesapeakes are.

WHEN JUDGING THE CHESAPEAKE BAY RETRIEVER
BY EDITH TICHENOR HANSON

Edith Tichenor Hanson judged the National Capital Chesapeake Bay Retriever Club Specialty Show in 1990. The Hansons were part of the active contingent of the American Chesapeake Club in the Bay area until their move to Roy, Washington, where the recently formed Evergreen Chesapeake Bay Retriever Club now has the benefit of their experience.

I approach the judging of all the breeds I do in the same manner. I always keep in mind the purpose of the breed and those attributes that allow or help a dog to perform the breed's original function.

In the Chesapeake, balance and size are very important. A totally balanced, well-muscled dog should be able to hunt all day or all week without breaking down. This also requires a dog to be sound. A proper size dog is essential. I wouldn't want to be in a boat in icy water when a one-hundred-plus pound dog is trying to get back in or when jumping out for that matter!

Proper coat is a unique feature to our breed and should not be excused away. It was developed with reason and must be retained.

Many exhibitors may not know that all judges approved by the AKC have signed that they will judge by the approved Standard for the breed. One need only study the Standard to see what is considered most important and judge accordingly. It sounds so simple, but all judging must come to compromises in the ring since we haven't found the perfect dog yet. How those compromises are arrived at makes the differences in judging we see today.

I would hope that all exhibitors would study the Standard and try to breed dogs to match it. It was written to describe a totally functional hunting companion; everything in it contributes to that end.

JUDGING CHESAPEAKE BAY RETRIEVERS
BY NAT HORN

Nat Horn wrote recently that he grew up with Chesapeakes and with the sport of dogs as a family hobby, showed in Junior Showmanship a few times, put a CD on his bitch Ch. Eastern Waters' Androscoggin, CD, but really didn't take a great interest until after he grew up. Nat has also trained Chesapeakes in Obedience and Tracking as well as the American Chesapeake Club Working Dog title. He is the only breeder-owner-handler of two different Chesapeakes who have won Best in Show.

One thing that my father often advised me of long before I started judging is how important it is to *look for what is good in a dog before you start to get concerned about faults*. It can prevent you from eliminating a dog from competition because of one minor negative thing, or from rewarding a dog who perhaps has nothing outstandingly wrong, but is a dog that in all aspects is quite mediocre.

Within breed type you find various kennel types. Different kennels excel in different breed characteristics and become noted for their positive attributes. Coats, head type and expression and degree of substance are just a few of the features that can contribute to kennel type. Dogs that lack breed characteristics and deviate from the Standard in this regard lack type and should not be labeled with breed or kennel type. These dogs are classified as off types.

One thing that has come up in discussion about dogs and Standards is the question of sex. Should dogs and bitches look the same or should there be other differences besides the specified weights and heights? I always thought this kind of thing was understood and not needed in the breed Standard. I expect a bitch to show beauty and femininity, and I expect that I should be able to recognize this before rear examination. Likewise, I expect a dog to be masculine, proud and distinguished. If a Chesapeake looks like the opposite sex, I feel this is incorrect and I fault this to the degree of the deviation. There is more of a tendency for judges to make the mistake of rewarding "doggy" bitches than to reward "bitchy" males. Judges need to be more cognizant of this.

During any discussion of the virtues of positive attributes over negatives, considering the whole dog is important. Getting off track and overemphasizing one aspect of the dog can lead to poor judging. In judging Chesapeakes, I like to refer to the phrase from the Standard under Symmetry and Quality, "the dog should be well proportioned," then judge all the component parts, relate them to each other and look at the dog as a whole. Throughout the Standard many traits are referred to with a phrase like "medium" or "moderate." I find it most important to keep in mind the places in the Standard where things are emphasized with stronger words.

Chesapeakes retrieve objects from the ground or in the water requiring a neck and head of well-proportioned length that combined permit the nose and mouth to reach the ground or grasp fowl easily in the water. The Chesapeake should not be restricted in the water or forced into a stooped position on the ground. The purpose and function of this breed of good proportion requires a well-balanced head.

In examining components of the head, I consider the following: a medium stop which implies that the Chesapeake should not be down- or dish-faced and the look should be clean. It should also have a muzzle that is pointed, but not sharp, gradually tapering to a pointed look at the tip. The muzzle should not be blunt, square, short or snipey.

In judging Chesapeakes, I fault overdone, cloddy dogs with excess bone and muscle that interferes with performance. The Chesapeake is equivalent to an Olympic swimmer or runner who has efficient power and agility with good muscle tone, and is not to be compared to the wrestler or weightlifter, overloaded with muscle but not able to use it efficiently as a swimming or moving animal.

I consider coat the most important breed characteristic. A dog who is out of coat or has a poor coat really should not be shown. I expect a thick, dense, short, wavy coat with a harsh outercoat and a wooly undercoat. One thing that I look for is coat on the sides of the dog. The dog becomes immersed in water and must have protective coat all over the body. The coat is to be thick and dense in places where it is straight and in places where it is wavy. The short, thick, kinky wave is more desirable than the wavy coats that are longer and softer.

The color of the Chesapeake is for camouflage in a working environment. These colors include all shades of deadgrass, and browns. Past Standards contained a disqualification for liver-colored dogs. I believe the attempt was to discourage breeders from breeding extremely dark Chesapeakes of a hue which appeared to be almost black. The extremely dark dog does not camouflage in the working environment and should be faulted.

I consider the term "severely penalized" comparable to the judge's action on a serious fault. A well-proportioned dog that is strong, balanced and well angulated can perform as the Chesapeake was intended to. Dogs should weigh sixty-five to eighty pounds, and bitches should weigh fifty-five to seventy pounds. An overdone, oversized, underdone or undersized dog in the ring has a serious fault. I still look at what is good about the dog and weigh it against the problem or problems. I have felt that judges often reward dogs that are oversized and/or overdone. It is appalling when dogs of good quality within the height and weight of the Standard lose to dogs that are oversized in one way or another because a judge has made awards for the wrong reasons.

Breed characteristics that will probably always have room for improvement include the coat, head and expression and the Chesapeake outline. Breeders and judges both need to continue to breed and judge by the Standard.

The most significant improvement in the breed has been temperament. It is evident that many breeders have concentrated on producing even-tempered, intelligent animals with ability, courage and a strong will to please and work. They are not machines, but are curious individuals who desire an understanding of what their owners desire. Owner and Chesapeake should develop into a remarkable team.

WHAT I LOOK FOR WHEN I JUDGE
BY BETSY HORN HUMER

Betsy Horn Humer was raised with Chesapeakes since 1946, for most of her life. She and her husband established a household in 1965, and their first Chesapeake was Ch. Eastern Waters' Oak, CD, TD, WD. Oak went on to win two National Specialty Shows and produce a total of 25 breed Champions.

As I look at the dog in the ring, the first thing I see is the profile or outline. The proper outline of the Chesapeake Bay Retriever is a unique and distinctive feature of the breed. The dog is to be slightly longer than tall, although the legs should not appear to be too short or dwarfed when compared to the dog's body. Any dog should be well balanced with front and rear angles matching.

Approaching the dog I see the head, which should also be in proportion to the rest of the dog and of proper size. The Standard calls for "medium." The head should not be oversized or overdone. Remember that if a dog is to carry a duck or goose, that dog's head should not be so big that with the added weight of the game the dog is out of balance. In addition, there should be a difference between the heads of dogs and bitches. You should be able to tell whether the Chesapeake is a dog or bitch by looking at the head. Bitches should not be "doggy"; less frequently, we see dogs with "bitchy" heads.

The proper coat can be judged by sight and feel. It is short and wavy. You can see if the proper dense, wooly undercoat is present, which will "push" the outercoat away from the body and give it a full appearance. To the touch there is a bouncy feeling. The correct outercoat feels harsh and crisp. I am not color-conscious as long as the coat is correct, and will blend with a hunting environment or surroundings. Because this is a short-coated dog, you can almost judge the Chesapeake with your eyes alone and do not need to do much "handling" other than checking the bite, shoulder layback and quality and texture of coat.

I especially look for some of the distinctive fine points that set the Chesapeake apart from the other retrievers: the high-set small ear, eye color that blends with the dog, hare feet and proper tail carriage level with the dog's back. In addition, the dog's rear may be the same height as the shoulders, or a trifle higher. This statement has been misinterpreted to mean that the Chesapeake should be swaybacked. *Even with a rear that is slightly higher than the shoulders, the dog's back should not be soft and sagging.*

After I've looked at these dogs standing still and examined them, then I hope they can move! You must remember that the Chesapeake was developed as a swimming retriever, and stifles are to be well angulated, which will provide for a strong swimmer. The front assembly of the dog should have adequate layback of shoulder to match the rear. The Chesapeake's side gait should cover a lot of ground in one stride so that the dog is also an efficient hunter in the field and will not tire easily. It is also important to remember that when a Chesapeake moves away from you, as speed increases, the legs tend to converge toward the center.

A word most often repeated in the Standard is "medium." The dog should not be overdone: The body should not be too long with legs too short, or with legs too tall with a short body. Keeping in mind that this dog is to sit in your duck boat and be able to climb in and out easily, this should not be a 110-pound dog.

Temperament is another criterion by which dogs are judged. Breeders are striving to produce Chesapeakes who are even-tempered with a happy disposition and an intelligent expression. A judge should be able to detect a willingness to work and an alertness. Chesapeake Bay Retrievers were not originally developed to be a ''show dog,'' but this function is becoming an important one. However, quieter, reserved dogs or, particularly, bitches should not be penalized. Chesapeakes can be slow to warm up to people. One cannot really judge courage or intelligence in the ring.

The intelligence, willingness and devotion of the breed are some of the qualities that make me want to be owned by a Chesapeake Bay Retriever. Ultimately, I am looking for the dog or bitch that I want to take home with me!

The King on the Kingstone!

6

Buying a
Chesapeake Puppy

CHOOSING A PUPPY should be thoughtfully done. This is no light matter, for you are investing in a companion for many years to come, so of course you will want to get the best puppy you can to suit your needs.

CHOOSING A BREEDER

First of all, do choose a reputable breeder. Try to find one recommended by the parent club, which is the American Chesapeake Club. Chesapeake owners find it well worthwhile to pay the moderate annual dues that entitle them to club membership, and to receive the six bulletins the club publishes each year. The bulletin discusses all breed problems, has articles on the latest health procedures, records the achievements of the dogs in shows, lists Obedience and Field Trials and all competitive and performance events and is an ever-welcome source of general helpful information. To become a member of the American Chesapeake Club, write to the current club secretary, whose address can be obtained from the American Kennel Club, 51 Madison Avenue, New York, N.Y. 10010. The American Kennel Club operates a breeder referral service, and only reputable breeders are accepted for the breeders listings in its monthly publication, *The American Kennel Gazette*.

If you are looking for a dog for your family and/or for hunting, you will obviously have a wider choice than if you are looking for a dog to show in conformation or Obedience, or to compete in Field Trials.

Different breeders specialize in strains particularly suited to one or another of these categories. But any Chesapeake should come from working stock. It is not enough just to be a fine-looking specimen; a Chesapeake should also work.

The trend in retrievers today is to keep them doing the job for which they were intended—retrieving. A dog who demonstrates a willingness and ability to work is a much more intelligent and pleasant companion than one who does nothing.

Any reputable breeder will not object to a prospective buyer asking legitimate questions about the puppies available for sale.

One of the things you should find out is if the puppy's parents have been X-rayed for sound hips, and having met the criteria, if they have been certified free of hip dysplasia by the Orthopedic Foundation for Animals. Chesapeakes are a hardy breed and, on the whole, eminently sound. But dogs of all large breeds—Great Danes, Saint Bernards, German Shepherd Dogs, Labradors, Goldens, Chesapeakes and the other retriever breeds—may carry genes for hip dysplasia, and the hereditary components of this disorder are not fully understood. The conscientious breeder makes use of X-rays and the diagnostic services of the OFA to aid in the selection of sound breeding stock.

In addition, both parents should also have a CERF certificate and number. CERF stands for Canine Eye Registration Foundation, which was started about 1975. A CERF number means the dog has been examined by a board-certified veterinary ophthalmologist and found to be free of such hereditary eye diseases as cataracts and progressive retinal atrophy, both of which can be inherited and cause blindness. Although Chesapeakes as a breed have a low incidence of these, the CERF number should be a requirement for each dog before breeding.

When you go to buy a puppy, have the owner of the litter show you the dam of the pups. If the sire is on the premises, take a look at him. Some breeders, if they do not own the sire and he is not available for viewing, will have pictures to show prospective puppy purchasers. In addition, try to see all the dogs the kennel has on hand. It has been said that the status of a kennel lies in the quality of its *average* dogs, not just in some outstanding individuals.

Breeders who are reputable feed their dogs properly, give them any

Litter owned by Leif Holm, Denmark.

necessary veterinary care and do not breed intending to make a profit. This is not true of the puppy mills, so be sure not to patronize such places. Taking care of a pregnant bitch involves special feeding, special vitamins and careful supervision of whelping. It also means constant observation of the progress of the pups after they are born. The female should be wormed when she first comes in season, and the puppies should be wormed at four to five weeks and again at six to seven weeks, to clear up any infestation.

A careful breeder gives the puppies supplemental feedings from some time in their third week of life, and usually they are weaned in the sixth to seventh week, allowing time for the immunities from the first inoculations to be fully effective. *No reputable breeder will ever let a puppy go to a new home without having been given "shots" to prevent distemper and other viral diseases.*

OTHER CONSIDERATIONS

Are both parents of the pup friendly and well adjusted? Do they retrieve with zest and enthusiasm? Ask if the dam and/or the sire has

Eyes open, just out of the nest: "What a big world this is!"

been used as a shooting dog, and if either of them has a Working Dog Certificate.

If you are looking for a show dog, inquire if the parents have been shown successfully. There should be bench champions in the pedigree. Do try to find a breeder who has more than a superficial acquaintance with shows and whose champions have been consistent winners.

If Obedience is your thing, ask if either the parents or the grandparents have earned any of the Obedience titles: CD, CDX, UD, TD or TDX. If possible, find out who trained and owned them, and if they were campaigned in Obedience after achieving their titles.

If you are looking for a Field Trial prospect, be sure to buy your puppy from a breeder with a record of success in retriever Field Trials. The pedigree of the puppy should contain the names of some of the current Field Trial Champions or Amateur Field Trial Champions. Remember that the dogs four or five generations back are not as significant an influence as the parents and grandparents.

In 1993 the going rate for a good puppy is $400 to $500. Special ''prospects'' may command higher prices. No, the breeders are not making more money or showing a greater profit. The cost of dog food has increased, and veterinary fees are higher because the vets find themselves with increases in overhead. In addition to these routine maintenance expenses, the breeder nowadays must pay for X-rays and OFA opinions (and if a dog does not prove fit for breeding, there is no refund to the

The first Chesapeake litter in Germany, with their dam, Karen von Low's Holiday Surprise.

breeder; failure costs as much as success). CERF eye examinations for all dogs are another necessary expense to be incurred by today's breeders if we are going to do it right.

CHOOSING A PUPPY

Most puppies are sold when they are seven or eight weeks old. A puppy should not be shipped under the age of eight weeks, and there are now regulations forbidding the airlines to accept them under this age.

When you are first shown the litter of puppies, carefully observe the attitude of the group as a whole. They should be happy to see visitors, and come charging up to the fence, wagging their tails and competing for attention. If there is one that is timid and hangs back, you would be well advised not to consider taking that one.

Do the pups, as a group, seem healthy and robust? What is the condition of their kennel run? Is it clean and sanitary? There should not be any unfinished food pans sitting around to attract flies.

There should be no dewclaws on the puppy's hind legs. Look at the pup's mouth. Teeth, at this early age, may be slightly overshot and will straighten out later on. A pup should not be undershot, meaning the lower jaw protrudes further out than the upper jaw, for this fault will almost certainly not correct itself.

Puppies should be well boned but not overheavy or clumsy. They should be active and well coordinated, and move effortlessly at a trot. Look for the sloping shoulder that gives reach in front movement and is balanced with a well-bent stifle providing driving power from the rear. What you see on land is indicative of what this dog will do in the water.

After you have decided which two or three you like the best, perhaps you may take them for a little walk so you can observe their reactions to new things and new places. When pups have never been given any retrieves, if you bring a golf or tennis ball with you and bounce it in front of them a few times, you will see which of them is the most alert. They also should show an interest in retrieving any ball that is rolled on the ground in front of them.

At Guide Dogs for the Blind, in San Rafael, California, many years ago Eloise Heller worked with Clarence Pfaffenberger and Stanley Head in devising puppy tests to help select the puppies that were most trainable and bold enough to do the work of a guide dog, and this program is still being continued at the institution. Retrieving was carefully observed, for it denotes the willingness of the dog. Also observed was the reaction of a small puppy to a loud noise. A pup should be startled by it, but should adjust to it.

If you are considering an older pup, remember that young dogs do not stop growing until they are a year old. They go through some awkward-looking stages until that time. The Chesapeake usually has attained full height at a year, but will continue to fill out and mature for at least another year or two.

THE BIG STEP

Okay! You have picked out a puppy that you like and you are satisfied that the people who own the litter were happy to answer your questions. They also impressed you with their sincerity, as well as the good quality of their dogs.

Before you leave you should be given a pedigree of your pup, as well as the registration certificate that you must send to the American Kennel Club in order to have the puppy registered in your name. If there are delays in AKC procedure and the certificate has not yet been received by the breeder, the breeder should give you a bill of sale that identifies the puppy by age, sex, sire and dam, as well as the date of transferring the puppy to you, the new owner.

You should also find out the feeding schedule used for the puppy, so that you can continue it, and ask what kind of food has been used; most breeders will volunteer this information, which is important for the puppy's welfare and smooth transition to new surroundings. Changing foods abruptly can be upsetting to a puppy's stomach. Small puppies should be fed three times a day until they are about three months old, then twice a day until between six months and a year. Some modern foods do not require supplementation, but you should follow the breeder's and then your veterinarian's advice as to whether or not vitamins, bone meal or calcium, cod liver oil and so forth should be added to your puppy's diet.

The breeder should also supply information on inoculations the puppy has had and when the next ones are due, the dates when wormed and when a stool sample should next be examined. This data should be given to your veterinarian so it can be made a part of the puppy's file the first time you take the puppy to the vet.

THE NEW PUPPY AT HOME

You will anticipate your puppy's arrival at home by preparing a box, basket or crate to use as the pup's bed. Of course this should be placed in a sheltered spot, out of any draft and not in the full sun where it may get too hot in the middle of the day. You should provide access to a space outside of this box that your new pup can use as "bathroom facilities." You will usually find dogs will not soil their sleeping quarters.

The first night away from littermates may be a lonely one. A clock or softly playing radio may give your pup the feeling that there is company nearby.

If you plan on keeping your dog in the house, housebreaking will only take a short time if you are careful about it. Put your pup outside in an enclosed yard *almost immediately* after every meal until the puppy has relieved itself. Praise and then bring the dog in for a while.

The last thing you do in the evening is let your pup out before being confined to bed. The first thing you do in the morning is the same—rush puppy out to the yard. If this is done regularly, your pup will very rapidly establish the habit of being clean.

When the puppy is to live in the house from the beginning, a crate is the best recommendation for a bed that will become the dog's den. For those lonely first nights, put the crate in your bedroom where you can reassure the dog or even reach out and give a comforting pat or two. Your dog can take naps, and even meals in the crate, and it will prove to be

Puppies and cows. Switzerland.

the solution for many of the problems that arise when raising a puppy to become a well-mannered dog.

SOCIALIZATION

Early socialization is important, and if you can locate a "Puppy Kindergarten," enroll your puppy, where you will both enjoy it as you learn.

When your pup is about three or four months old, if you are interested in training, you should contact the American Chesapeake Club regional director for your state and find out if the club has a Training Day scheduled. In areas where the club is very active, these Chesapeake Days may be held every month, but in other parts of the country there may not be more than one or two a year. In this case the regional director may be able to offer an alternative, or direct you to a retriever club holding training sessions for owners of all retriever breeds.

INTRODUCTION TO RETRIEVER TRAINING

Properly introducing a young dog to water is very important. The novice should be started in wading water, and after satisfactorily per-

"Chowder" playing "E. T."

forming in that, the retrieves can be gradually lengthened so that the dog has to swim a little. As a pup becomes more confident, you can give retrieves that are *only* in swimming water.

Never make the mistake of throwing your dog in the water—you can ruin the dog for life. Hold the reluctant dog on leash, while watching other dogs retrieve. Most dogs have a very competitive spirit, and they will want to do the same thing. You can even let two dogs go after a bumper at the same time. The practice days of the Chesapeake Club usually involve retrieving birds as well as bumpers. But again, your dog's introduction to feathers should be carefully done and be supervised by a knowledgeable person.

It is good for any young dog to go to such classes, for they become accustomed to seeing groups of people and other dogs. It definitely makes your dog a better adjusted pet as well as a better hunting dog.

If you are going to have your dog professionally trained, be sure to inquire about the "pro" you are considering. Some trainers dislike Chesapeakes, and if they do they will not give them a break. By judicious inquiring you should be able to locate a trainer who likes Chesapeakes as well as Labradors and Goldens.

A lot has been written about individual outstanding Chesapeakes. Many have had phenomenal wins in the shows. Quite a few have gained

A new view of the world.

outstanding records in Obedience competition. And the successful Field Trial Chesapeakes are well known from one part of the country to another.

But we tend to overlook the hundreds of Chesapeakes who are, in their own way, the most important of all—the average hunting dogs who also serve as the family pet. As Lorraine Weremeichik reminds us, "We must not forget the importance of the dog who lives within the family, giving them the love only a Chesapeake can give. The dog who is, day after day, part of the family life. The dog who will, on the days that you are feeling down and out, do some silly thing to let you know that he is there and cares. If they sense danger, these dogs stand ready to defend those they love. In addition to being the children's playmate and pet, they are eager and ready when father calls to go hunting—no matter how cold the weather, the water or the snow."

7

Teaching the Chesapeake Puppy

by Mildred G. Buchholz

T HE STRONGER you build the urge to please in a puppy, the easier the teaching is going to be for both you and the pup. At first there is no reprimand; the teaching is in the form of fun games. This helps to build the desire to please.

Dogs can be taught on two levels of learning: the conscious and the unconscious. Learning on the unconscious level is the learning that pup does without being aware of learning. The pup is repeatedly put into a situation and this is duplicated so many times that the dog reacts over and over the same way. Learning on the conscious level is when a pup is shown what you want. You give the command and the pup finds out what your language means by trial and error, and will soon associate the action with the command.

The good part about all this teaching is that the trainer does not have to be smart. Let's face it, there are some sad humans teaching smart pups. The smart pup will take advantage of the teacher! I've been called an evil person by some of my friends and that may be so, as I just love to see a smart pup take advantage of the teacher. This is where I find out just what kind of person the trainer is.

If the trainer stops the lessons, this smart pup will start doing the training. I've found Chesapeakes are notorious for this. However, the

Millie Buchholz with 15-year-old Chesachobee's Rocket. Millie grew up with Chesapeakes on the eastern shore of Maryland, and had them all her life, starting her Chesachobee Kennels in Florida where her enthusiasm and understanding have extended to breeding, showing and every area of training for Obedience, Tracking and Field. Those who knew her would say, "Millie can talk Chesapeake."

way is easy if you will use firmness along with affection in teaching a lesson. Make sure the pup understands what you want by starting the lesson over. This will build the confidence the dog has to have in the teacher. The person who really learns to teach is the one who can figure out the situation and approach a problem from a different angle. If the desire to please is developed in a pup at an early age, the desire to work will be a reward when the dog gets older.

Scientists have discovered by tests of litters that no one pup in a litter is actually smarter than the other. However, they have found that one pup takes responsibility faster and learns better, and responsibility does have to be learned. A pup has to have the right environment to develop a sense of security, and the best time to develop this is from eight to twelve weeks old. By removing a pup from a litter after about eight weeks, giving a pleasant home and protecting the puppy from harm, that dog will become secure. Also, it is a good idea for you to take your pup different places and make sure to socialize with other dogs and new environments as well as new people.

Regardless at what age you get a Chesapeake, remember that teaching is understanding and trust in the teacher. The trust is a two-way deal;

Beaucrest Bosco Rock at eight weeks. This boatsman grew up to make his TD at the age of six months and three days, and CD at one year. He is owned by Debbie and Jim Heitman.

it is equally important that your dog trusts you and that you believe in your dog.

TRAINING AFTER TWELVE WEEKS

At about twelve weeks of age a conscious level of learning can start and play lessons can change to let a pup know he or she is being taught. These lessons do not abruptly change; you just make sure your dog does what is expected.

Step by step you will add new things, but remember, don't lose the trust. Don't assume what your pup knows, but instead go back to the ABCs and do simple things. If a pup learns that you like her to carry and

Kiana cooling off in her own pool. Age twelve weeks.

bring things, there will be no problem in the future when you throw something to be retrieved.

Most pups will pick up whatever they can get in their mouths, so it is important to never discourage a pup from retrieving. You must praise the dog for fetching by taking the object gently and with praise—a secure pup is a happy pup and a happy pup will take lessons easily. Teach the pup to retrieve several different objects: tennis balls, puppy bumpers or small paint rollers, which I like to use when the pup is cutting new teeth, as they are soft on the mouth.

I have a friend who bought a pup for a companion, and in her backyard were many pine trees, hence many pine cones, so the pup learned to carry and retrieve pine cones only. She was a retrieving fool for pine cones. Then came the day when my friend decided she wanted to enter a working test. We went out in a soybean field to train, and as the bumper was thrown, this retrieving fool was sent, marked it, went straight to it, left it and ran like a crazy fool all over the field looking for a pine cone—back to the drawing board with this one.

One phase that some dogs go through involves retrieving only what they want, such as the case of the pine cones. They are only expressing their independence, and as in all other teaching, this phase will pass. But you must not wait for it to pass; don't let the dog train you. In most cases I have found this to work well: I slow down on my training periods and shorten them to three to five minutes. But during this time, I see to it that the pup does everything I ask of him by making the requests simple.

Robin Brennan's puppy, Rascal, retrieving through goose decoys.

After being a retrieving fool for pine cones, toys, balls and so forth for weeks, then not picking up a bumper, dumbbell or bird when thrown, the Chesapeake's basic inborn desire to retrieve comes to your rescue—that is why I always start a pup on play retrieves. The toy (pine cone, toy, ball) is your secret weapon in this case. This way you will not lose trust, nor do you put pressure on the dog.

A TRAINING SCHEDULE FOR PUPPIES

First day: Hold the toy in your hand and let the pup smell it, wave it around until the pup is about to die to have it thrown, then put it away out of sight.

Second day: Do the same as above, only this time throw the toy; pup retrieves with no problem. Give lots of praise, then put the toy away. Out comes the bumper. Throw it, and the dog starts for it but stops—no soap. Just stop and put pup away and then go pick up the bumper or object you wanted the pup to retrieve.

Third, fourth, fifth and sixth day: Follow the same procedure as above, but only throw the toy once each day. In a week's time the pup will want another retrieve so badly as to retrieve anything else you throw that he doesn't particularly like, and will turn out to be a retrieving fool on anything you send to be picked up.

If you don't lose your cool, and don't give in to the things that the dog likes (remember only one throw!), it will make the bond stronger between you and your pup.

A TRAINING PHILOSOPHY

My reason for this type of training is that it works with most people if they will work each day for just three minutes. Other methods are either nagging or too much pressure, and some dogs can never be brought back to look truly happy by the average person. Sure, they will retrieve, but in the long run, with most people, they will never be the dog they would have been if they hadn't been nagged or pressured. Some of the trust has been lost with more severe methods.

Your voice and tone are the means by which you communicate with your pup regarding what to do. You may think because a pup does not understand sentences, talking to him or her is crazy. Your tone, mood and actions affect everything when the dog is with you. Don't be a fool and try fakery by using an artificial tone. Your dog is smart enough to know whether you truly mean it, or are just using empty words, and it looks to your tone of voice for an understanding of right and wrong.

If you believe what I have told you, then teach your Chesapeake all that it can be, and in the end you will have a happy, secure, trusting, outgoing adult dog.

MISTAKES MOST OFTEN MADE BY OWNERS

1. Using the dog's name for a correction instead of "Awp," "Ak," etc.
2. Not giving pup sufficient play before and after lessons so the dog will enjoy the lessons.
3. Giving too little praise. Remember the pup learns through praise and success. Help your pup to be right and avoid corrections.
4. Not giving the pup credit when using intelligence.
5. If a correction must be given, make sure that praise is given with the correction, so that you don't lose trust.
6. Nagging—both voice and lead nagging.

Rascal, fully grown, retrieving a full-sized Canada goose.

7. Not concentrating, and anticipating how the pup will react.
8. Incorrect timing of praise. Remember, praise should be given with the command and not after the pup has completed the action. This is the thing that has most fooled trainers.

"Tempo" clearing ice. Chesapeakes play and work in water with equal enthusiasm; it is never too cold, for it is their natural element. This is Wild Mountain Chesapeakes' foundation bitch, Chesrite's Wild Mountain Tyme, CD, WDQ, owned by Mark Kaufman and Linda Allington.

8

Chesapeake Character— One of a Kind

HUNTERS CONSIDER the Chesapeake to be *the* truly all-around hunting dog, and their descendants have maintained a loyalty to the breed that will keep the Chesapeake on the American hunting scene. With changing conditions ever increasing the limitations on hunting, the great breed character of the Chesapeake has refused to be denied, and the breed is becoming more widely known and drawing to it a host of new devotees eager to pursue interests in every appropriate field of canine endeavor.

The Chesapeake is an all-around dog, and a personality in its own right; it has long been recognized that each one is an individual and responds to individual treatment. They have an inherent quality of self-respect and their own worth. They are intensely affectionate, sensitive and perceptive. "I think these dogs have *deeps*, that other dogs don't have," an English kennel maid said, and it is true that they are not only highly intelligent but also possessed of a variety and intensity of feeling that gives them almost human personalities.

They are deeply devoted to owner and family, and very possessive. With the pride of possession goes a strong sense of responsibility; the Chesapeake is a natural "watchdog" and children's guardian, ready to protect home, family and property. "They are home-loving dogs," said Jim Cowie, the great retriever man. Yet this dog is not unsociable, and welcomes the owners' friends, who become the Chesapeake's friends, too.

The temperament of the breed has been criticized by some who do not understand it; each dog breed has an individual character and not every individual exemplifies the ideal. The Chesapeake has flourished as proof that careful breeders are successfully producing good temperaments. Active, intelligent and "busy," a Chesapeake needs the stimulation of training and work to do to channel energy away from mischief, and to develop intellect; the Chesapeake is happiest as a member of the family, sharing family activities when not sharing the hunter's companionship afield. For many who have known the companionship of a Chesapeake, there can be no other dog.

Nancy Lowenthal grew up with Chesapeakes, and wrote: "Chesapeakes are at their best when part of a human family. When they enjoy this privilege, they will work long and hard. Although accepting confinement reasonably well, they cannot accept a solitary state devoid of people; they need, and must have, love from humans.

"This dog is serious about work and responsibilities. An understanding, fair, loving (though demanding) taskmaster will receive unsurpassed loyalty and devotion. Chesapeakes are inclined to ignore strange people and animals as long as they do not interfere with what the dog considers

Am. Can. & St. Ch. Nuka Bay Toklat, WD, Am/Can CDX, St CD, meets "Easter Birdie" the cockatiel. "Tok" was bred, owned, trained and handled by Lynda Barber.

the proper performance of duties, one of which is to protect family property, real and otherwise, including house, lot, acreage, cars, trucks, children, dogs, cats, birds—anything that the dog considers worth protecting. Chesapeakes do not need to be taught to protect property; it is instinctive. A wise owner will not encourage this propensity, but will control and channel it.''

Chesapeakes are dogs whose devotion and loyalty usually are completely given to owner and family, and often they are indifferent to other people. They are one-person dogs and many will not work well for anyone but their owners. Or, if they do, it is not with the same degree of enthusiasm. Perhaps this is why professional trainers seldom do well with them.

Chesapeakes are somewhat disinterested in other dogs and are usually only tolerant of them. Chesapeakes are not usually fighters unless the other dog starts it, but will take no nonsense from other dogs, and give an excellent account of themselves once a fight starts. Puppies should be discouraged from fighting, as when they are young it is easy to discipline them. Nothing is a worse nuisance than a scrappy dog.

CHESAPEAKE CAPABILITIES

Those of us who believe Chesapeakes to be the best all-around dog feel they have many capabilities we like to stress:

Family Dog Par Excellence, happiest when really a part of the family. This does not mean they must live indoors, but rather that you attain the best cooperation if your dog is one of the family group. If allowed in the house even for short periods, the dog feels like a part of the family. Chesapeakes will follow children about all day, meanwhile watching over them. Babies and toddlers can, and often do, annoy and pester a pup or dog, and if the going gets a little too tough, the dog will get up and move out of range.

However, it can be unfair to leave a dog to the toddlers' tender mercies, and *young children need to be taught to respect the animal's rights* and to show their affection through kindness and gentleness. Protectiveness is a trait of our breed and a family with a Chesapeake is pretty safe from intruders. If intruders come, they surely will leave quickly! After a time of riding in the family car, it becomes the dog's car, too. If you leave your dog alone in it, you need not lock the doors; it will be guarded for you.

Hunting dogs are what Chesapeakes were intended for, and they

Wildwood's Pretty Penelope obeys "Mush" for three-year-old Katie Jo Rollins.

excel on land as well as in water. The Chesapeake will find all your dead birds, and seldom loses a cripple. An experienced hunting dog has a tendency to retrieve cripples first—for in a short time they might hide or swim away. After delivering the cripples, your dog *then* goes for the birds that are dead, and this really helps to conserve game and fill out bag limits.

When Cliff Brokaw began to run Labradors in Field Trials, he still kept a Chesapeake that was his hunting dog. Although quick to admit that the dog was "no good for trials," he boasted in mingled pride and astonishment that "he always knows where the birds are." This was a very intelligent dog who knew how to open the kennel gates, and he used to let himself out and stroll up and down the line, deciding which of the Labradors he would let out that day to go for a walk with him.

Knowing where the birds are is innate in Chesapeakes of the best hunting strains, and these dogs need scarcely a modicum of experience for this talent to manifest itself. I know, for I had one in my first Chesapeake, who was richly endowed with the quality defined as "bird sense," as well as being the ideal all-around dog and family companion.

Nancy Lowenthal credits this story to Charlie Sambrailo: "One cold, drizzling, ordinary-duck-hunting-weather morning, Ed Fleischmann and Snuffy Beliveau took big, old, friendly Ch. Bayberry Pete out to the duck club for a day's shooting. It was necessary to travel in a small motorboat from the clubhouse to the blind. Pete had a dim view of motorboats and repeatedly tried to jump out. He soon was thoroughly convinced by Snuffy and Ed that "STAY" meant stay in the boat as well as stay on the line, and sat disconsolately, but obediently, in the boat's bow. The boat suddenly hit an underwater berm and threw both men into the water. Not Pete, who remained in the boat where he had been told to stay. The boat bounced off the berm, turned and, with motor still on, made its way back eventually to a place near the clubhouse dock with Pete still firmly ensconced in the bow. When the keeper discovered the boat, Pete decided to be "on guard," as Chesapeakes usually do with their owner's possessions. Unable to get into the guarded motorboat, the keeper took the remaining boat, which had no motor, and rowed slowly out to rescue the stranded, cold, wet, disgusted hunters." (Chesapeakes take orders seriously and well when they have been impressed to do so. Sometimes too well.)

FC/AFC/CFTC Nelgard's Baron, CD, always an exciting dog to watch, was purchased from Monroe Coleman by Cliff Brignall. After Eloise Heller had successfully run Baron in several trials, Cliff was persuaded to sell him when he was seven. With Eloise, Baron came into his own, as one of the most outstanding Field Trial contenders of all time.

Another story illustrating Chesapeake nature came from Monroe Coleman, the original owner of FC/AFC Nelgard's Baron, CD, the sire found most often in the pedigrees of today's best Chesapeakes. Monroe took the very young Baron hunting to grounds about five miles from his home, on a poor day for duck shooting. It was late morning before the hunter finally shot down a very high flyer. Unknown to both Monroe and Baron, the bird landed in a channel and drifted some distance from where they had seen it go down. Baron hunted in vain and finally was called back to the blind. Monroe lined him again to the original mark, and again Baron returned with nothing. Monroe, enraged about the loss of his only duck, recast the dog for the third time and got into his truck and drove home, leaving Baron to his own devices. That evening, after dinner, Monroe relented and started out the door to look for Baron. On the doorstep sat Baron with the duck on the doormat. It had been nearly seven hours. The development of this natural perseverance and intelligence led to Baron's becoming one of the truly great retrievers of his day.

Babysitter   When I first met Bob Ray, he told me, "I was raised by a big Chesapeake bitch," and this is another aspect of Chesapeake character. My youngest son was inseparable, in his preschool years, from our bitch Tallapoosa who was just two weeks younger than my son Roger. Tally grew up and raised puppies and carried on a public career in the shows, and she was one of the family and very close to all of us. Roger and Tally were four years old when we had a pond dug so we and the dogs could swim without leaving home. Roger was the only nonswimmer and he played in the shallows while the rest of us swam in deep water, and Tally was always at his side and never left him.

On other occasions, if one of us went to swim alone, Tally accompanied that person into the deep water and swam around, never getting more than a few feet away. She was our self-appointed official lifeguard. Roger, when the older children were away at school, often told me, "I'm going out to play with Tally." I never knew what all their pastimes were, but one game was for the child to put the Chesapeake on a Sit-Stay, run and hide a toy or a ball on the other side of the house, out of sight, then return and release her to go and find it, and of course she always did, but the most impressive thing was the way she did her part in sitting and waiting until she got the command to hunt and retrieve. There was no way this child could enforce obedience, and the Chesapeake knew it; she played the game his way because it pleased her to please him.

As **Devoted Companions** no breed can beat ours. Although they accept society as a whole, their idea of heaven is to spend their time with you, and many of us must agree with Eloise that "no day starts well for

"Cubbie" smiling.

me without my morning greeting of the Chesapeake 'smile.' It is most gratifying and flattering when you first see your Chesapeake in the morning, with tail wagging, rump wiggling and lips laid back from the teeth, giving you that horrible grin stemming from an intense delight to see you again. You cannot fail to be both amused and flattered. May I always start my day like this!''

After a day of hunting. FC/AFC Ed's Turnpike Drifter, owned by Vince and Lottie Shetzler.

9

The Chesapeake: Hunter and Versatile Companion

$\mathbf{D}$IFFERENT METHODS developed in duck hunting on the Chesapeake Bay, and the unlimited abundance of waterfowl called for guns that could not be used today, such as the "murderous swivel gun" employed by "old Varnell," who shot ducks for Canton's owner Dr. Stewart at Sparrow's Point. Canton was old Varnell's hunting companion, her patience and endurance of fatigue seemed almost incredible, and "on one occasion she brought out twenty-two or twenty-three ducks, all killed or wounded by Varnell at a single shot."

LITERARY REFERENCES

The big guns of the market hunters were described by James A. Michener in *Chesapeake* (Random House, 1978):

Duck hunting with a big gun was an exacting science best performed in the coldest part of winter with no moon, for then the watermen enjoyed various advantages: They could cover the major part of their journey by sliding their skiffs across the ice; when they reached areas of open water they would find the ducks clustered in great rafts; and the lack of moonlight enabled them to move close without being seen. The tactic required utmost silence; even the crunch of a shoe on frost would spook the ducks. Sometimes it took an hour to cover a quarter of a mile; the barrel of the gun was smeared with lampblack to prevent its reflecting such light as there might be.

With one explosion of a big gun like this, the watermen sometimes got themselves as many as eighty or ninety ducks. On rare occasions they would be able to fire twice in one night.

Describing such a gun, Michener says:

It was one of the proudest guns ever to sweep the ice at midnight. It was a monstrous affair, eleven feet six inches long, about a hundred and ten pounds in weight, with a massive stock that could not possibly fit into a man's shoulder, which was good, because if anyone tried to hold this cannon when it fired, the recoil would tear his arm away. The gun was charged with three quarters of a pound of black powder, over a pound and a half of Number Six shot, plus one fistful.

This gun was mounted in a fourteen-foot skiff with an extremely pointed bow and almost no deadrise, chocks occupying what normally would have been the main seat, and a curious burlap contraption built into the stern area. The gun barrel was dropped between two chocks, a wooden lock was secured over it, and then the heavy butt was fitted into a socket made of burlap bagging filled with pine needles in the stern area. You don't point the gun; you point the skiff. And when you get seventy, eighty ducks in range, you put a lot of pressure on the trigger. The gun explodes with a power that seems to tear a hole in the sky. The kickback is absorbed by the pine needles in the stern.

The gunner's Chesapeake was then expected to retrieve all these birds. Another waterman "mounted seven guns in his boat, each with a barrel two inches in diameter. They fanned out like the tail of a turkey gobbler. There was a trough just below the powder entrances to the seven guns. It was filled with powder all the way across the trough, and it was lit at one end. It then fired each of the seven guns in order."

In celebrating the eastern shore, Mr. Michener sometimes seemed unaware that there were two sides to the bay. The Chesapeake Bay's celebrated ducking grounds were upon its western shore, or Baltimore and Harford counties, within the area bounded upon the north by the Susquehanna River and on the south by the Patapsco River. In our time, as in Michener's, the government owns practically all of this shore line. The Weiskittels' place at Marshy Point is almost the only one of the old ducking shores remaining in private ownership.

DUCK SHOOTING AT THE BAY

In the old days, the duck shooting began at the head of the bay, opposite to Havre de Grace, upon the flats in the middle of the bay's head

74

basin, where the notorious "sink-box" shooting flourished in bygone days. On the southwestern edge of the flats is Spesutie Island, then Mosquito Creek, Romeny Creek and Abbey Point at the mouth of the Bush River. Across that stream is Gunpowder Neck. The Gunpowder River is a stream that has always been considered to furnish the finest duck shooting on the Chesapeake Bay. The south shore of that river is Middle River Neck, containing Grace's Quarters, Marshy Point, Bengie's and Carroll's Island—the great clubs whose records go back to the early 1800s, as told by Ferdinand C. Latrobe writing in 1941, in *Iron Men and Their Dogs*. These records were lost when the Weiskittels' house burned down at Marshy Point, and this was before our time.

All of these places were first noted for their "shore blinds," wherein the ducker waited for the birds to swim onto the baited ground before his blind. They were known, too, for "point" and "bar" shooting at the ducks, which with express-train speed, skirted around the "point blind," or flew high over the "bar." Every Baltimorean of sporting inclination aspired to ownership of, or membership in, a "shore"—which still means anything from an extensive acreage to a hundred feet of waterfront with blind privileges.

The Bartletts and Haywards owned three ducking shores, besides stationing their yacht *Comfort* upon the Susquehanna Flats as a mother-ship to their sink-box rig. In the 1880s, Bartlett, Hayward & Company built its only ship, the side-wheel steam yacht *Comfort* that they used to tend their "ducking rig" for sink-box shooting on the Susquehanna Flats. After her launching, the partners decided that the *Comfort* was too small for their widely extended hospitality, so the vessel was sawed in half and an additional section was constructed in the shops and put between the forward and after sections.

William H. Lafflan in 1877 described a visit to a ducking shore on the Bush River, arriving after a two-and-a-half-hour drive behind a pair of "trotters," to be surrounded by a host of dogs whose hospitable barks awakened the ducks bedded down in the Bush River, some four hundred feet beyond. Lafflan's first experience of duck hunting began with awakening at three o'clock in the morning, and after a hearty breakfast, the duckers boarded a batteau. Guns and cartridges were put aboard, and as the host picked up the oars, he let several Chesapeake Bay dogs settle among them for the row to the blind on the point. As the boat entered open water, they paused at sight of a "tremendous rick—must be ten thousand ducks in it," and Lafflan saw two Maryland duckers shoot into an impenetrable void, marking the falls of three unseen ducks. They sent two dogs who slid from the boat and swam off in the black water, returning in a few minutes with the game. Waiting in the marshgrass-

Chesapeakes raise head and shoulders out of the water to locate their objective as they swim.

thatched blind was chilling and uncomfortable and Lafflan had lost his enthusiasm for Maryland ducking when dawn broke and the flights of ducks began to come up the river and into the decoys, bunch after bunch of Canvasback and Redheads, allowing hardly time between them to retrieve those brought down from that ahead. The sight intoxicated Lafflan: "I was excited; I was wild, and I began to mark invisible ducks myself. 'Good sport,' I repeatedly declared." By nine o'clock they had ninety-six fine ducks in the blind.

His host being a "big gun man" displayed the supreme art of "bar shooting" at a little flight of Baldpates racing at express speed directly over the blind, so high in the air they resembled pigeons, with a "No. 4," a man-high, nineteen-pound gun calling for extraordinary marksmanship. As he followed the birds and brought down three of them, the dogs leaped into the water simultaneously with the Baldpates stumbling in the air. Over these narrow peninsulas, ducks crossed at terrific speed, high in the air, and consequently the huge "No. 4" guns, with a bore almost as big as a quarter, loaded with thirteen drams of black powder and several ounces of shot, and with a range of over one hundred yards, were required to reach the birds.

The logbooks (covering some sixty years) of the unrivalled Gunpowder River clubs contained very, very few one hundred-duck days. The consistent ducker's average day, when shooting over decoys, was only about seven ducks in the fall season and six ducks in the spring. In the sink-box shooting upon the Susquehanna Flats, however, the bags did frequently approach the category of slaughter.

THE CHESAPEAKE'S ROLE

This was ducking on the Chesapeake Bay in the nineteenth century, and such a sport could not have flourished without the aid of the strong, sound, intelligent, water-loving dog with the desire to hunt and retrieve, the ability to use eyes, nose and common sense and the determination to bring back whatever the dog was sent to find, no matter how long or difficult the search. There are many stories of Chesapeakes disappearing for hours, sometimes overnight, and some having been given up for lost before they return with their birds.

Years ago we lived where ducks sometimes came to a little pond in the woods behind our house, and late one afternoon my husband took his gun and one of our Chesapeakes, and was lucky enough to down a duck that disappeared among the trees. He sent the dog; the dog veered and went in another direction, and as it was growing dark, he called the dog and came home. Early the next morning they set out again and the dog again indicated a direction where the bird could not possibly be, was soon out of sight and in minutes he was back with the duck that had been shot the evening before. Chesapeakes have always been noted for finding and retrieving cripples while leaving the dead birds for later because they weren't going anywhere.

A hunter without a dog loses cripples, and the first time Fred Dalrymple took his Chesapeake to the Jersey shore he proudly reported back that he had got so many brant or black ducks, "and Traveler, he got him a goose." It is not unusual in those marshes for a dogless hunter to abandon the search for a crippled bird, and for another hunter's dog to pick up the cripples and lost birds later on, and Traveler became very good at this, as well as never failing to retrieve the birds shot by his owner.

Eloise Cherry has a story from a century ago in Nebraska, of a billfold containing money and valuable papers being lost during a day's hunting. Back at the clubhouse was a big, beautiful Chesapeake dog, and his owner borrowed a handkerchief from the distraught hunter, and talked to the dog as one would to a person. He said, "Mike, this man has lost his billfold and you must go find it," as he had Mike smell the handkerchief. It was dark as ink and raining, and the hunter said there could be no possible chance for a dog to find that billfold. Mike did not return that night, but the next morning he was lying on the top step of the bunkhouse with a billfold between his paws.

Isabel Owen's Ch. Water Witch, CDX, would never let her down and was one of those Chesapeakes who appear to understand every spoken word. After a long day of training in the field, Mrs. Owens looked to see if it were time to go home, and discovered that her watch was missing. She turned to Water Witch and said, "Tater, I've lost my watch," and the clever and devoted Chesapeake set off at once, and searched the training grounds until she found and returned with the watch.

The Hursts in their Chesacroft Kennels brochure, published in 1925, told of one of them leaving the point blind to take refuge from a sudden storm in a little cabin nearby. He left the rubber cushions that he used for a seat covering in the blind, and continued on back to the house. That afternoon at feeding time one of the young puppies being trained that day was missing. Early the next morning when Mr. Hurst returned to the point, he was greeted by a fierce puppy growl followed by hilarious and happy barks of welcome. That seven-month-old puppy, who incidentally became Ch. Chesacroft Tobe, had stayed, without a word of command, without food and by his own will, faithfully guarding his master's property.

When we got our first Chesapeake, almost everyone who recognized the breed had a story to tell, and one of the first was of a family who had left their Chesapeake in their car when they went Christmas shopping, returning to load packages into the car and going to shop for more, until they came back to find a small crowd gathered around their car and a very unhappy stranger with his hand inside the car and his wrist in the Chesapeake's mouth. The man was unharmed, as the dog held him gently but with such firmness that he could not pull his arm away, and none of the spectators was so foolhardy as to interfere, and the dog would not release the intruder until his family came back and he could turn the responsibility over to them.

Another acquaintance of the breed told us with awe and admiration that one of these dogs had "saved a human life." The story was of a pleasure party out on a boat with a Chesapeake among the passengers; a child fell overboard and none of the partying people were aware of it, but the dog instantly jumped into the water, grasped the child's clothing and held the child afloat until rescue could be effected. A documented instance of a similar kind occurred in 1924 when the two-year-old son of Dr. Lloyd Lewis was pulled from an icy stream by a Chesapeake named "Sonny," who belonged to Harry Weiskittel. It was snowing hard; the tot wandered to the water and broke through the ice. The dog dragged

Hunting buddies. Robin Brennan's Chesapeake would work as a nonslip retriever at heel while the setter works ahead of the gunner to find the game. After the birds are shot down the retriever goes on command to pick them up.

the child, Dick Lewis, from the water to the roadside and left him there. Sonny went to the house and made it known that help was needed.

The Hursts had a permanent blind at Legos' Point, and here their dog, Prince of Legos (the sire of Ch. Chesacroft Tobe) was accustomed to lying alongside the blind about on a level with their heads. Little attention was paid to him as he lay still as a log. His occasional tremors were attributed to the cold and soon forgotten in a spasm of shooting, until they began to notice coincidence between these tremblings and the shooting that generally followed, and commenced to watch the old dog. He would sight a duck at much further distance than their eyesight permitted, and his eyes would never leave it. From that time on the watching on the riverside was left to Prince, and the owners contented themselves with watching the dog, knowing that his incredible eyesight would not fail them.

"Hunting with a properly trained Chesapeake," wrote the Hursts, "you will know the acme of sport. And you'll find this is more than a dog—a Chesapeake is a most intelligent pal."

DOGS FOR DEFENSE

In 1942, William E. Buckley, who later became president of the American Kennel Club, organized Dogs for Defense, a voluntary civilian

A perfect water entry! UCDX Rockrun's Millie of Beaver Lake, CDX, owned, trained and handled by Valerie Farrell.

Eastern Waters' Fearless Cub, CDX, owned, trained and handled by Charlene Petrolino, demonstrating equitation on the family farm.

agency that encouraged dog owners to offer their dogs to the armed services to be trained for various kinds of war work. Most of the trainers were dog people, of course, and we met some of them after the war. The German Shepherd Dog breeder Bernard Daku, who had liked the Chesapeakes but in most cases found they were unsuitable for attack training, said: "It proved too difficult to make them vicious; they are such happy dogs." What a tribute to Chesapeake temperament!

The Chesapeakes starred in other ways, notably as Sentry Dogs accompanying a serviceman on sentry duty, for with their keen senses and alertness coupled with the protectiveness that make them such wonderful watchdogs, they readily developed a partnership and were invaluable aids to sentries who could always rely on the warnings given them by these dogs.

DOGS IN SERVICE TO THE LAW

Eloise Cherry sold Pruneface to a game warden who found hunters hiding illegal birds in the hubcaps of their cars, and he trained the dog to sniff at the hubcaps of each car, and Pruneface became very proficient at sniffing out the hubcaps. This was long before "sniffing dogs" came into general use for the detection of drugs and explosives.

The first Chesapeake I knew to be used for drug work was Chesachobee's Donner, TD, bred by Millie Buchholz and owned and trained for Tracking by Carole Borthwick. Carole's husband was a police officer in Florida, and his other dogs were German Shepherds. Working Donner in the K-9 program, he found the Chesapeake to be superior in many aspects of police work, and could not have spoken with more pride when he told me how good Donner was at "smelling out dope."

More recently, Ch. Pond Hollow Scoutmaster went from the Homespun Kennels of Marie Guthier to the Pennsylvania State Police, and was stationed at Swift Water Barracks in the Poconos where he worked at drug detection until his retirement.

The proud owner of Eriez Sir Thunder Thor is Detective I Richard D. Heismeyer of the New Jersey State Police, who reports, "Thor was my dog before training, and only because of another dog failing out of the canine academy did I bring him down to be trained. Thor was five years old when he began narcotic training . . . he is now nearly ten years old and going strong." One of their jobs is to go to schools and show the students what a narcotic detector dog can do, slipping in a message about the dangers of drug abuse without the kids realizing it. Most of the schools

New Jersey State Police Detective Richard D. Heismeyer and "Thor." Handler with his narcotic detector dog.

invite them back year after year, and ''everyone wants to see 'the dog.' '' Trained to alert to marijuana, hashish, heroin, cocaine, crack and methamphetamine, Thor has been responsible for the confiscation of nearly $3.5 million in U. S. currency, and over $3.5 million worth of illegal narcotics. Weekly training searches and periodic attendance at seminars maintain their proficiency at a high level, and in 1989 competing with police and military teams from all over New Jersey in the first annual Narcotic Detection Competition, held at Fort Dix, the team of Rick Heismeyer and his Chesapeake Thor was awarded a first-place trophy.

CHESAPEAKE GUIDE DOGS

In 1942, Guide Dogs for the Blind was established on the West Coast and soon took its present quarters at San Rafael, California. When William Johns, formerly of the Seeing Eye, came to head the new organization, he had owned and hunted over Chesapeakes for many years. As a result, he proposed to try one as a Guide Dog. From 1953 to 1959, twenty-five Chesapeakes went out with blind people as their Guide Dogs. These dogs were intelligent and their sense of responsibility was outstanding. They were quiet and they made excellent house dogs. The blind people really liked them. The one flaw that many of them seemed to develop was that they became too protective. As their devotion to their masters grew, they became overprotective and often would not let other people come near them, in some instances even wives or husbands. This, obviously, created a difficult situation in the family, on streetcars and buses and in job situations. Because of this overpossessiveness, Guide Dogs for the Blind was obliged to discontinue training Chesapeakes for this work.

THERAPY AND ASSISTANCE DOGS

New frontiers are opening for Chesapeakes as therapy and assistance dogs, and it is a most rewarding way to share our dogs' companionship and feel that we are performing a uniquely worthwhile service at the same time. In 1986, Jeannie Kinney took steps to work with Therapy Dogs International and began a program of regular visits with her Chesapeakes to the Ancora State Psychiatric Hospital in South Jersey. ''Clients who could not be reached by any other means have been communicated with through the dogs, and loud and aggressive clients change when the dogs

"Piedmont," working Canine Companion Service Dog in California.

arrive and become gentle and patient while waiting their turn.'' Jeannie's dogs were Obedience-trained, and she and the therapist were successful in teaching the necessary Obedience commands to younger clients who wanted to walk the dogs and do so in an orderly manner. When these Chesapeakes arrive at the hospital, ''as if in the field, they would start to cry and whine and become excited as if they can't wait to get to their work. Their selflessness with patients is inspiring, and no matter how unresponsive a patient is, they are always trying with a gentle prod of their nose and a wagging tail.'' Recently, Joanne Silver in northern

New Jersey has fallen under the spell of doing therapy work with her Chesapeake, and is very actively encouraging others to enter this field.

AT HOME ON THE FARM

Chesapeakes are always eager to help their owners, and many have made themselves useful and taken responsibility for livestock beyond simply acting as watchdogs on farms. Dr. Brenda Stewart's first Chesapeake showed her this natural proclivity, and she taught him to help turn a herd of thirty-two Holsteins out to pasture in the morning, and go gather them up at night.

Monica Mance's assistant gardener, Ch. Grandpaw's Chowderbay Putsch.

Ranee Nevels is raising sheep in Tennessee, and her Chesapeakes are quite expert in helping to herd and care for the stock. My first Chesapeake, Glory, was a puppy when she began to round up our hens and herd them back into the hen yard from whence they had strayed. This was not a dog chasing hens for fun, this was serious work, and once inside the fence where they belonged, she was satisfied to go about other business. When a next-door neighbor's hens invaded our yard, Glory would harry them until they retreated to their own side of the hedge that divided our properties, but she herself never crossed the line. Escaped hens would "steal nests," and at times our supply of eggs would noticeably diminish. One day my husband said, "Glory, where do you suppose those hens are hiding their eggs?" She disappeared into an outbuilding, and came back with an egg in her mouth. After that it was always her job to go with us to gather eggs and show us any that were hidden. She was expert at mouthing the eggs without breaking them.

Glory's pedigree showed that her grandsire was Bill Holden's Big

Big Chief, Bill Holden's great gun dog and Field Trial contender, was the model for this half-century-old decal.

Chief. Big Chief was an Open all-age dog, and "Doc" Parrott considered him to be the greatest gun dog ever produced in his area. When we went to visit him at his home near Dover, Delaware, the Holden family were gathered in the backyard where Big Chief was leading around a freshly washed white pony that was to be shown that weekend. Although he was eleven years old, the big dog was happy to show off by jumping a hedge to retrieve a dummy. This was a Chesapeake that had his place in the family. "He had more sense in that big head of his . . . ," said Isabel Owens; and in Field Trials and hunting he fulfilled the purpose of his breed and enjoyed the closest companionship with his master. His life gave him everything a Chesapeake could ask for.

Chesapeakes are also great watchdogs because they do not just bark at nothing, and they will always let you know when anyone comes onto the property. Pay attention when your Chesapeake tries to tell you anything; don't scold your dog for making noise without first investigating the cause, and you will have a reliable and trustworthy guardian.

Am. & Can. Ch. Suegartree's Flying Cherry, CD, JH, WD, owned by Deloris Shirmer, is from the last litter bred by Eloise Cherry.

10

Training Your Hunting Dog

by Eloise Heller Cherry

HUNTING WITHOUT A DOG just isn't any fun for those of us who have been lucky enough to shoot over a well-trained Chesapeake. It really isn't very difficult to educate your dog—and it can be great fun. There also is satisfaction in knowing you will conserve game when your dog can be counted upon to bring in all the birds you shoot. Chesapeakes are determined dogs and they persevere in their search for cripples.

Several thousand Chesapeakes are kept as a combination hunting dog and family pet. Actually it is an ideal arrangement. There is no reason why your dog can't be the children's playmate, a household guardian and an excellent performer in the field. It is really up to you. If you go about it properly, it is easy to have an eager and obedient hunting companion who happily retrieves all the birds you shoot.

Chesapeakes are natural retrievers, and you will see this trait clearly exhibited, even in puppies who may only be six weeks old. Throw a ball in the pen with some very young puppies, and in no time at all you will see them competing for it, and one of them carrying it around in its mouth. You often will see a puppy chase a leaf that the wind has blown by, pick it up and carry it around—just for fun.

Caroway's Kiela, MH, WDQ, bred and owned by Carol and Jon R. Andersen, was the first Chesapeake bitch to earn the title of Master Hunter. Kiela produced three qualified all-age dogs and three Master Hunters.

You certainly want to encourage this instinct, for after all, that is what your dog is meant for, to find and carry to you the birds you shoot.

Of course, the best hunting dogs are those that have been properly trained. But there is no reason why the average hunter can't train his or her own dog if willing to expend a little time and energy.

We do not *train* as much as we *teach* a young dog.

Ch. Poisett's Starboarder Morgan, CD, MH, WDQ, and his son, Ch. Wild Mountain Colonel Crockett, MH, owned by Mark Kaufman and Linda Allington. Morgan earned Derby points, scored high in Obedience, and is the sire and grandsire of Master Hunters. Crockett is Mark's best hunting buddy and qualified for the 1991 Master National.

FIRST THINGS FIRST

A definite time should be set aside each day for you to be with your puppy, even if it is only for fifteen or twenty minutes. You should work with your dog in a place where there are no distractions, such as loud noises, other dogs or people passing by.

You start by putting a choke collar on your puppy; attach a leash to that and put the dog on your left side. Give the command "Heel," pat your left side and encourage to come along with you. After your pup is moving with you in a satisfactory manner, and you have given praise for

Deep Fork Dock Rock, MH, owned by Paul Clayton II. "Doc" is the youngest Chesapeake to be a Master Hunter.

this cooperation, stop training until the next day. You may have to do this several days before you can move on to the next command, "Sit."

To teach the "Sit," on leash of course, you gently force the dog's rump down with your left hand, meanwhile pulling up a little with your right hand, which is holding the leash. Praise extravagantly when your pup does it well. Then combine the two commands "Heel" and "Sit." Again be sure to praise enthusiastically—"Good dog! Good dog!" Do not make your training sessions too long, and play when you are through working.

The next command is "Stay." This is an enormously valuable word, with all kinds of practical uses. After you have heeled and have told your dog "Sit," then introduce the word "Stay," while still on leash, of course. Move away and say "Stay." Then return and again say "Stay."

You should be able, in a few days, to circle while the dog stays motionless. When this is going well, discontinue the lesson and end up by playing.

The distinction between work and play is basic. You are *insisting* on working, and you should praise often and should be loving but firm. Following work time, a puppy must also have a separate play time that is fun.

The next command your dog must learn is "Come." I prefer that word to "Here," because "Here" and "Heel" sound so very much alike. Have the dog "Heel," "Sit" and "Stay," and while still on leash, give the new command "Come." When you do this you gently pull toward you and back up a little bit. When your dog comes to you, give a world of praise, so the dog will enjoy coming to you.

Now, in an enclosed spot, do all of this off leash. Disobeying any of these commands means putting the leash back on again, and making the dog do it properly.

RETRIEVING

Not every amateur is successful in forcing a dog to retrieve. I personally think that if you have a willing retriever, you can teach "Hold" the boat bumper or dumbbell, and this should be sufficient for the average hunting dog. If the bumper is dropped, put it back in your dog's mouth, close the lips over it and make the dog hold it while you heel on leash. This should give the idea that the dog is not to drop it. When hunting, if your dog drops a crippled bird, and the bird starts to get away, that alone should teach "Hold." Be sure that you are teaching your dog with bumpers, *not* with birds.

I must repeat that you should be generous with your praise and keep your training periods short so that you do not lose your dog's attention. "Stay" is the command you will later use when you start to teach your dog double retrieves. It is also the command you will use when you teach steady to shot.

"No" is an extremely important command—with innumerable handy uses. It should be said in a harsh and unpleasant manner. It really means "Stop immediately what you are doing." Sometimes it even means "Don't dare do what you were thinking of doing." Like wetting in the house, or chewing up a shoe, or thinking of fighting. The command "No" could, and often should, be accompanied by a swat on the dog's rump, just for emphasis.

MOVING ON—DOUBLE RETRIEVES

When your pup or dog is retrieving properly on a single, bringing it back to you, sitting at your side and releasing the dummy on the command "Out," you can then, but not before, start to teach double retrieves. But do not overlook the importance of cooperation on the command "Out," or "Give." No tug-of-war here, please. You don't want to do anything to make your dog "freeze" on the bird, which is the expression used when a dog will not give the handler a bird. The new plastic small boat bumpers are the best to use. The old-fashioned canvas bumpers, filled with feathers, have the drawback that most dogs like to "pop" them. This may cause the habit of biting into the bumper and subsequently biting into the bird, which will surely make them unfit to eat.

After single retrieves are being smoothly performed in the yard, you should get someone to go into a field with you and throw the bumpers for you, so that you can increase the distance of the falls.

Ch. Nordom's Chelsea Legacy, CD, MH, WDQ, the first Champion Master Hunter Chesapeake bitch. Bred, owned and handled by Norene Szechenyi of Nordom Chesapeakes.

But when you start to teach double retrieves initially do them on the lawn or in the open, so the dog can see both falls. Throw the first one, and say "Stay," then throw a second bumper. Naturally you send the dog for the last bumper thrown. Say "Come," and when the dog comes to you you, say "Heel," and make the pup come to your left side. Say "Sit," and "Out," and after you receive the first dummy, you then send your dog for the other one. It sounds complicated, but it really is easy. If you can train with some Field Trial people, they can demonstrate it for you, for all Field Trial dogs, even those in the Derby, have to do double retrieves.

In Field Trials the dogs are sent to retrieve by calling their names. Many hunters just use the command "Fetch," which is okay as long as you and your hunting buddy don't both say "Fetch" and send both your dogs at the same time. In that case, the result could be a glorious dog fight.

When you commence doing double retrieves, have the bumpers fall about 180 degrees apart. Then the dog will have to come by you with the first bumper before going for the other. This gives you the chance to call your dog to deliver before you send for the second fall. Some upland game hunters don't bother to train their dogs on doubles, as they feel they will probably only get one shot. But duck hunters often get a chance to shoot two, or even three times, if a flock comes in to the decoys. So a duck dog would benefit by learning to do double retrieves.

WATER WORKS

When you start working on water, pick a warm day. It is ideal to take your pup to a pond with an older experienced dog. At first it should be wading water, and the puppy should be allowed to just play in it, but after a short time will probably start following the other dog into the deeper swimming water. The pup should set the pace here.

Then give the older dog a retrieve in deep water, and you usually find that the pup will follow and start to swim also. First retrieves should be short ones, where the dog can run in for them. The distance should be gradually lengthened each time. Although Chesapeakes are wonderful water dogs, never throw a puppy or dog into water. A dog could easily become water shy, and be afraid of water for a long time.

Introduction to feathers is very important. Pheasant or duck wings should be used at first. Then progress to dead birds. Then, live birds that are shot for your dog. Last would come shackled ducks. Avoid discipline

Tori's leaping water entry earned her high scores in Style.

on birds; do not give your dog any birds to retrieve until you are completely satisfied with the performance on bumpers.

Securing birds with which to train is not easy if you don't know where to go. If they are having a Chesapeake Day in your area, by all means attend it, for they will shoot pigeons and also have live shackled ducks for the water marks. They also will have some experienced people there to coach beginners. You will meet other Chesapeake owners, and as your dog improves, be able to compete in the Hunter's Stake. Bring your family and a picnic lunch and make a day of it. Your dog will become accustomed to a crowd, and also, to working when there are other dogs around.

BEHAVIOR MODIFICATION

If your dog growls at the others, or shows any tendency to fight, stop it right now. Give an unpleasant jerk with your leash and collar, and a stern command "NO." If that does not work do not hesitate to use a willow branch and give several cracks on the rear end, accompanied by several more hard "NO"'s. A fighting dog is not only a nuisance, but is also dangerous to have around. Don't stand for it for one moment—stop it immediately!

If you want a "perfect" dog, be sure to send your dog to a trainer who likes Chesapeakes, for, unfortunately, not all trainers do. Your local American Chesapeake Club regional director should be able to help you select someone with a good reputation and one who is not too hard on the dogs. People think of Chesapeakes as tough dogs, but most of them respond much better to an affectionate trainer than to a handler who is tough with them.

A CHECKLIST FOR HUNTING DOGS

"Snuffy" Beliveau, a famous Western retriever trainer, is very emphatic on a refresher course before the hunting season starts. He feel you should:

1. Harden up your dog if not regularly exercised.
2. Check obedience—"Sit," "Stay" and "Come."
3. Work on live game, even if you can't shoot it until the season opens. Go to fields where there are pheasants or quail. When your dog flushes them, shoot a blank pistol, or just shoot in the air, and check if the dog is steady to shot. If there are no fields near you where game can be found, buy some pigeons and take them to a field where you can work your dog on them.
4. If you have had trouble with your dog chasing rabbits, try to go into an area where rabbits are plentiful. Then if your dog chases them, you must discipline severely. It is wise to do this before the hunting season starts.
5. Put a leather collar with identification on your dog's neck so that if lost, your dog can be returned.

Tattooing a dog's ear or flank with a number or name, if properly done, is a positive means of identification. But the fellows who steal and sometimes sell hunting dogs take the dog first and inspect later. If they discover a tattoo, they will want to get rid of the dog quickly.

At the end of a day's hunting, Beliveau also advocates checking out your dog for any foxtails or burrs. Look over feet carefully, to be sure there are no thorns of foxtails between the toes. If so, they should be promptly removed. Also check ears. Avoid a lot of discomfort for the

Ch. Pond Hollow Spindrift, CD, SH, WDX. "Drifter" was bred by Dyane Baldwin, and owned by her and her husband Bill. Dyane trained and showed him in conformation and in Field, and Bill trained and showed him in Obedience.

Birmingham Lady Victoria, MH, WDQ, with owner-handler Daniel DiFrancesco. "Tori" was the only Chesapeake bitch to complete the 1991 Master National, and the youngest of all-breeds to complete. She has licensed Field Trial honors and is competing at the all-age level in licensed trials.

dog and a veterinarian bill for yourself. If eyes are red, or look irritated, use a little 2 percent yellow oxide of mercury, easily obtainable from a drug store without a prescription, as it is often used in babies' eyes.

Weekly brushing is advised, and an ordinary scrub brush can be used to remove the dead hairs in your dog's coat.

THE CHESAPEAKE—BEST AT HOME

You should have a properly enclosed place in which to keep your dog at home, a dry, draft-free doghouse on a platform raised from the ground. A run should contain some sun and some shade.

The proper place for your Chesapeake is on your premises, guarding your house and family. You certainly don't want your dog roaming around the countryside to easily get run over or poisoned.

The fact that a large, impressive-looking dog is on the premises is a great deterrent to trespassers or possible thieves. Dogs have an uncanny instinct about people's motives, and even the friendliest of dogs seem to sense when an intruder does not mean well. A low growl from a big, tough-looking dog is usually sufficient to discourage any intruder.

After all your hours of working together your dog is undoubtedly devoted to you, and would be miserable without you. You have, ahead of you, many fine years of companionship as well as fun in the duck blind or in the hunting field.

11

Hunting Tests for Retrievers

by Leslie A. Lowenthal

HUNTING TESTS are made to order for Chesapeakes. The Chesapeake's desire and determination are ideal for the tests, which simulate actual hunting situations. Neither rough terrain, cold or turbulent water, mud nor poor weather conditions will deter a good Chesapeake, which was developed as the primary hunting dog for the early market hunters and sports enthusiasts of the East Coast. This powerful, balanced dog with a harsh double coat relishes tough hunting conditions; the tougher they are, the better the dog likes it.

The precision and speed needed for Field Trials are not needed for the noncompetitive Hunting Tests, which are designed to evaluate retrievers rather than to eliminate them from competition. Our breed is made up of one-person dogs that do not train as well as other retriever breeds do with professional trainers. Extremely loyal, they are most responsive to training and handling by their owners.

Hunting tests were a long time coming. In the 1940s, after World War II, the only real retriever field competition was in the AKC Field Trials. These Field Trials were, for the most part, restricted to owners who could afford professional trainers. The average hunter with a good dog really could not compete. In addition, most perceived the trial tests and the white jackets on the gunners, throwers and handlers as contrived and artificial. Hunters always try to camouflage themselves when shooting ducks, geese or upland game so that they are not readily visible to birds.

FINDING THE RIGHT DOG—THE EARLY DAYS

Hunters had difficulty finding puppies of good hunting dog stock. The breeding of retrievers with Field Trial ability continued to be important, but the breeding of retrievers primarily to compete in dog shows was becoming increasingly popular. None of the prominent Chesapeake breeders wanted the separation of Chesapeakes into either field or show types. They had witnessed this type of separation in other breeds like the Irish Setter and even the Golden Retrievers and Labrador Retrievers.

AKC pedigrees noted only Field Champions or Amateur Field Champions. Many great retrievers never achieved titles and their superior hunting abilities could not be identified in pedigrees. If the hunters did buy puppies from the Field Trial breeders, they were sometimes too high-powered to be suitable hunting companions and their conformation, color, size and markings were often off standard. Field Trial retrievers were bred primarily for performance in trials.

Hunters couldn't find potential hunting dogs from show breeders because most of those breeders only bred to dogs that did well in the show ring, with little attention to whether their breeding stock had a natural desire to retrieve birds, enter the water or hunt game birds.

The national breed clubs became aware of the increasing division between show dogs and field dogs and determined to try to keep both field abilities and adherence to the breed Standard in all breeding stock. They wanted retrievers to look and hunt as they were originally bred. Some of the retriever breeds tried to make show championships contingent on passing certain field tests, but the AKC would not accept those limitations.

Pioneers of Dual Dogs

In the 1960s, Eloise Heller Cherry and Helen Fleischmann, both past presidents of the American Chesapeake Club (ACC) as well as prominent and successful breeders of Chesapeakes, started the Chesapeake training days. Both had bred and run Field Champions (FC) and show champions (CH) and had owned and run a few dual champions (FC/CH) and were devoted to maintaining a dual purpose breed. They wanted

Ch. Berteleda's Souvenir of Stoney, MH, WDQ. Bred, owned, trained and handled by Les and Nancy Lowenthal.

to make Chesapeake owners aware of the hunting instincts of their dogs and to instruct them in training their own dogs. These events were highly successful and very well attended. They were always enjoyable and the owners loved them. Eloise had started the ACC Regional Director Program and the regional directors (RDs) were encouraged to hold training days. They were soon held nationwide. They often included tips on showing dogs in Obedience and the show ring as well as field training.

In the late 1960s Working Dog (WD) Stakes and Working Dog (WC) Certificates were conceived and held by several retriever breeds to help identify dogs with the basic instincts of retrieving game birds on land and water. However, because of the simplicity of the tests, good nose, memory, perseverance and innate desire to retrieve birds were not always evident. Since WC and WD titles soon appeared on kennel pedigrees but were not permitted on AKC pedigrees, it was still difficult to identify field working predecessors. Although WD stakes, WC stakes, gun dog stakes and singles marathons were common, there was a real need for genuine hunting style testing.

NEW RETRIEVER TESTING

It wasn't until the North American Hunting Retriever Association (NAHRA) started in the 1980s, that there was any new style of retriever testing. ACC president Charles Sambrailo, who preceded me as ACC president, asked me to check to see if it would be worthwhile for the ACC to join this new organization. It appeared to me that this would be a noncompetitive way for Chesapeakes to earn field titles that could be included in pedigrees. Not many dogs, even excellent field dogs, could earn titles through the highly competitive Field Trials. NAHRA tests were simple and sound enough so that the average hunter could train his or her own dog for them. Many retriever owners flocked to the NAHRA tests, especially those opposed to Field Trials. The AKC, seeing this major movement toward hunting dog testing, joined hands with NAHRA and for a short time combined forces. Since NAHRA accepted crossbred and nonregistered dogs to run their tests and the AKC is primarily a purebred dog organization, this was a union that could not and did not survive long. Since the ACC is an AKC member club, we could no longer support NAHRA. The AKC and NAHRA began holding separate tests. Then the United Kennel Club (UKC) jumped on the band wagon with their own style of testing: the Hunting Retriever Club (HRC). All three organizations' tests were similar.

By 1985, some AKC Hunting Tests were being held. In January 1986 the AKC asked the ACC to participate in a seminar in the Los Angeles area. Charlie Sambrailo, Ron Foley and I attended this demonstration. It was a gala affair, held at the swank Coto de Caza, and was a big success. The AKC officers, field representatives and the editors of both the AKC-published *Gazette* and *Hunters' Whistle* attended. ACC member Jack Hansen showed and explained his new AKC Hunt Test video, "Love 'Em, Hunt 'Em, Test 'Em," in the club house. The local retriever clubs were well represented and the tests were well received.

The AKC asked the ACC to hold one Sanctioned Hunting Test to qualify the ACC to run Licensed Hunting Tests. The ACC held this AKC Sanctioned Hunting Test in April 1986 at Coto de Caza, with Leigh and Arnie Smith as secretary and chairman. Charlie and I judged the Master and Senior Tests, and Ron Foley and Mike Hautz judged the Junior Test.

Three Master Hunters bred by Carol and Jon Andersen. Caroway's Kiela, MH (far right), is the dam of Rosebud Rover Rendezvous, MH (left) and Caroway's Trick or Treat, MH (center). "Buddie" and "Trixie" are littermates.

The AKC wanted qualified judges and Ron and I had already judged the first AKC Licensed Hunting Test on the West Coast, held in Eureka, California on August 23, 1985, by the Redwood Empire Retriever Club (RERC). Charlie and I also were qualified to judge AKC Field Trials.

The first American Chesapeake Club AKC Licensed Hunting Test was held at Bong Recreation Area, Burlington, Wisconsin, on May 17 and 18, 1986. Dick Schultz was chairman. Ron Reed put on an AKC Licensed Hunting Test in Franklintown, Pennsylvania, on August 6 and 7, 1986, and through him our club became affiliated with the Northeast Federation for Hunting Retriever Tests, a group headed by Guy Fornuto, which was interested in furthering this growing sport.

At the 1986 ACC annual meeting held in Truckee, California, at the Field Trial Specialty, Charlie Sambrailo gave a glowing report on the AKC Hunting Test program and requested that more regions conduct these tests. Since Ron Reed successfully held his first Hunt Test in Pennsylvania in 1986, there has been one held there every year. Shirli and Chuck Hayes also saw the many advantages of the tests and began hosting AKC Hunt Tests in the Denver area. Ron Foley, Rick Schulke and I do an annual test in the San Francisco area of Northern California. AKC

Hunting Tests have continued to be popular and are now held in many areas of the United States.

THE HUNTING TESTS

The **Junior** Hunting Tests can be passed even by ordinary hunting dogs with minimal training that have inherited natural retrieving ability.

1. The retrieves are all singles.
2. Dogs are not required to be steady but must retrieve to hand.
3. Two land retrieves and two water retrieves are required.
4. No test should be over one hundred yards long, although some terrain may demand a little more distance.
5. Junior dogs do have to bring back live shot birds in good-enough shape for the table.

Breeders and owners with little field knowledge can run dogs with good natural hunting ability and receive the AKC field title Junior Hunter

Ch. Mitsu Kuma's Pond Mist, CD, JH, WD, was the first Champion Chesapeake to qualify in a licensed AKC Hunt Test. "Pistol" was bred by Dyane Baldwin and Barbara Mullen, owned by Dyane and Jennifer Baldwin, and trained and handled to all titles by Dyane.

Left to right: Farallon Feather Detector, CDX, JH, WDX, TT, and Ch. Winchester's Humboldt Gypsy, CD, JH, WDX, multi-titled Chesapeakes owned by Lisa van Loo.

(JH). This concept in itself is worth the whole effort. Many of these owners are encouraged to train their dogs further and to challenge the Senior and even the Master tests.

The **Senior** Hunting Tests are more difficult than the Junior Hunting Tests and require considerable training. These are not easy tests. A dog that completes a Senior Hunter title (SH) would be the equivalent of the best of hunting dogs for the ordinary hunter.

Senior dogs must:

1. Retrieve double land and water birds.
2. Be steady.
3. Honor while another dog is working.
4. Do two blind retrieves, one on land and one in the water.
5. Be taught to take a straight line without seeing a bird fall.

6. Handle on land and water.

7. Sit quietly and watch another dog retrieve birds.

The jump from Junior to Senior is a huge one. The Senior is probably the most difficult to pass. The judges are usually not as experienced as those in the Master tests and the testing is not always sound.

The **Master** Hunting Tests require:

1. A multiple (two birds or more) retrieve on land.
2. A multiple water retrieve.
3. A multiple combination land and water test.
4. The dogs to be steady.
5. Dogs sent to retrieve only once.
6. Recasts or controlled breaks not allowed.
7. Both land and water blind retrieves.
8. If there are double blinds, the dogs always be under control.
9. At least one retrieve to be a diversion bird, a bird thrown after the dog has left the line or is returning after being sent for another bird.

The Master Hunter (MH) requires just about a PhD in dog training. It is tough enough to do the requirements, but as these tests are simulated hunting situations, one must experience hunting conditions that seem unusual to the handler. There is a great satisfaction in qualifying in any

Wild Mountain Morgan's Moxie, CD, MH, owned by Mark Kaufman.

Master test because you know that you have a superior hunting companion. The dogs have improved so much since the beginning that experienced Master dogs are able to do satisfactory work under almost any condition or test. They are good, solid, well-trained hunting retrievers. This, of course, is what is desired.

Now a person interested in buying a retriever for hunting can readily identify sires and dams of suitable hunting strains because hunting test titles are included in AKC pedigrees.

THE MASTER NATIONAL

I was privileged to be a judge at the first Master National. The AKC had realized that after dogs had attained their Master Hunter title (MH), they were no longer competing in the Hunting Tests, and devised the Master National Stake.

With the required number of qualifying Master scores in the year previous, retrievers could compete in this advanced stake and continue to

Caroway Brown Bear Gunner, MH, bred by Carol Andersen and owned by Mark Kowalczyk, qualified and ran the 1991 and 1992 Master Nationals, and was a finalist in 1992. He started his show career with a win in his first show.

run each year that they met the requirements. Four qualifying scores were required in 1991. This was a concept done in the Field Trial Nationals and had also been done as sanctioned national type hunting tests held by the Northeast Federation and The Wisconsin Retriever Club with the Upper Midwest Flyway Federation.

The first AKC Master National was held in September 1991 at the C and D Canal Retriever Trial Area, near Glasgow, Delaware, and was hosted by the Del Bay Retriever Club. There were ninety-eight retrievers entered, ten of which were Chesapeakes. Twenty-six retrievers finished with qualifying scores; six were Chesapeakes. Chesapeakes had the best percentage of qualifying dogs finishing. The tests ran six days under the AKC Hunt Test rules. The Master National was a success and the Master National Retriever Club was formed to conduct these tests each year. The 1992 Master National was held near Nashville, Tennessee, and it was agreed to continue these functions across the U.S. in four geographic areas. Many of the same dogs ran in both 1991 and 1992, so it was assumed that the owners liked this concept and it would be continued.

JUDGING HUNTING TESTS

Initially the majority of participants attending the AKC Hunting Tests had little or no experience in Field Trials. Since there were no experienced hunting test judges, the AKC devised a category and point system. This system is cumbersome and time-consuming. It requires numerous computations that may cause errors and omissions. Both judges must agree on whether or not a particular dog has a passing score.

Originally the score sheets had categories for marking, style, nose, perseverance and trainability. The dogs were judged on a scale of 1 to 10 in each category with a passing average of 5. The average of the combined categories had to be at least 7 for a qualifying score. The "nose" category was dropped after the first advisory committee meeting, not because nose wasn't important, but because it couldn't be judged properly in relation to the other categories.

There is apprehension that the hunting tests will become too competitive. This competitiveness is a kind of American tradition and does creep in through the handlers themselves. Many handlers compare their individual score sheets to see who has the highest marks. Perhaps these tests should be scored pass/fail. The AKC is adamant at this time to preserve this noncompetitive attitude. This could change. The handlers themselves must make the effort to preserve the hunting tests as they were designed.

Ch. Rocky Creek's Blame It on DU, JH, WD, owned by Bill Shakley who trained and handled him to hunting and working titles, and shared conformation showing with his breeder Janice Bykowsky.

Judging clinics are given by the AKC, the Federation and various clubs in an effort to make the judging more consistent. The tests should resemble situations from a normal day's hunt. The judges give scenarios to justify and explain tests. The tests now are becoming less tricky with more normal evaluation of the dogs' abilities. As long as the Hunting Tests don't resemble Field Trial stakes, where placements are necessary and tests are challenging rather than appraising, there is hope that they will remain suitable for the average hunter.

LOOKING FORWARD

The future is a worry for those who wish that the Hunting Tests can continue in their present vein. They do what they were meant to do. They provide a place where the average hunter and interested amateur can run a retriever to be proud of in an enjoyable, camouflaged-clothed, noncompetitive atmosphere, and not have to worry about being overwhelmed by professionally owned and handled dogs.

Field and Bench Champion Sodak's Gypsy Prince, the first Chesapeake Dual Champion, was bred by Father Joseph Shuster and owned by Anthony A. Bliss. Prince was the forerunner of the modern Field Trial Chesapeakes, all of whose pedigrees trace back to him.

12

An Explanation of Field Trials

Based on work by Eloise Heller Cherry

ENGLAND, in 1900, was the scene of the first retriever Field Trial ever held. Each subsequent year these events became more popular. Many Americans visiting abroad attended them and were intrigued. However, it was 1932 before the first American trial was put on by the Labrador Club—for Labradors only. In 1933 the American Chesapeake Club followed suit and held one for Chesapeakes only. It was 1934 before an All-Breed Retriever Trial was held in this country.

Every year since then the number of trials held in the United States, and the number of competing dogs, has steadily increased. This tremendous increase of interest and participation has changed the whole character of American Field Trials—today they are somewhat of a rat race. Judges are not given enough time to adequately evaluate their fields. Unfortunately, many of today's tests are tricky ones that do not concern themselves with the dogs' innate abilities.

In England, Open entries are limited to twenty-four dogs, with two alternates, and this is done by a draw system. Also, their Field Trials are only permitted to be held in the fall, during the regular hunting season. Game is shot as it is flushed in the field, and they shoot whatever is encountered. The bag may be pheasant, grouse, partridge, snipe and an occasional duck, often a hare. For the English people would think it

Dual Ch. & AFC Mount Joy's Mallard was Ed and Helen Fleischmann's favorite dog. Mallard was trained by Rex Carr, and besides being a good marker, ran a fine diagonal "Carr" line.

highly unsportsmanlike to throw and shoot birds. They would feel that the bird did not have a fair chance.

American Field Trials often saw a professional run four, five or (on the East Coast) even eight or nine dogs. For judges to put on tests, in a three-day period, that adequately separate such a field is almost impossible. Dogs are often dropped from the first tests for any small error they might make, while in the later tests, the same fault may be overlooked in the winner or placing dog performance. Definitely, something must be done to cut our enormous and unwieldy entries.

If a dog "broke" (or "ran in," as they say in England), that dog was eliminated, as he was supposed to wait until the judge called a number and the handler sent the dog for the bird. This is also true today, as is elimination for "hard mouth."

In our early trials, when ducks were plentiful, they were shot from a boat, falling into tules or weeds. Live decoys, attached to weights, were used. But the dog who brought back one of these decoys was through for the day. The early handlers prayed that the guns would make a clean kill, for a live decoy and a crippled duck that was swimming in the decoys could easily be mistaken for each other.

Often an American handler had two dogs, one on each side. The judge would call the number of the dog to be worked. Meanwhile, the handler's second dog was expected to sit still, be quiet and just watch. It took a lot of training to obtain such control and discipline.

American trials are very different today—more complicated, and the dogs are supposed to do a tremendous number of different kinds of tests and combinations of tests.

Again, certainly, the average hunter would not expect a dog to retrieve a bird that has been hit, and sailed out some two hundred yards before it landed, without the dog even seeing the fall. But in Field Trials the dogs must be trained to do this. This type of test is known as a "blind retrieve." The dog must take a line toward the bird for a considerable distance, stop if the handler whistles and take arm signals to the fall. This test is often set up so that the dog has to cross a number of obstacles on the way (such as a deep ditch, swim through a pond and run through a heavily scented field) before reaching the place where the bird has been hidden.

Dual Ch. & AFC/CFTC Baron's Tule Tiger, CD, bred, owned and always handled by Eloise Heller. Tiger owns the top record of 208 all-age points.

Dual Ch. & AFC Meg's O'Timothy, CDX, owned by Joyce and Bud Dashnaw, was an exceptional dog who excelled in Field Trials, on the bench, and in Obedience. "Timmie" was trained and shown in Obedience and conformation by professional Doug Bundock. Timmie's great attitude brought him many fans gathered at ringside to watch him work.

All of these things, and more, are required of the Field Trial dogs of today. These dogs have more than a college education. They are PhDs!

Naturally, if you are interested in participating in Field Trials you would be foolish to buy anything except a dog that comes from good Field Trial lines, which have proven their trainability. The pedigree should contain the names of some of the recent Field Trial champions and other dogs who have proven their worth by winning places in the various stakes.

Anyone interested in Field Trials can write The American Kennel Club, 51 Madison Avenue, New York, N.Y. 10010 and ask to receive a copy of the two booklets that they have on this subject: *Field Trial Rules and Standard Procedures* and *Standing Recommendations of the Retriever Advisory Committee.* These publications discuss in detail all Field Trial matters, and a beginner should become familiar with them before starting to run a dog.

Today the regular stakes at a retriever trial are the Derby, Qualifying, Open All-Age and Amateur All-Age. We will discuss each in detail.

116

DERBY STAKE

The little book (commonly referred to as the "bible") says, "A Derby Stake at a Retriever Trial shall be for dogs which have not reached their second birthday on the first day of the trial at which they are being run."

For the benefit of beginners I will describe the test normally held in this stake. For many years the usual sequence was to start with a land single, followed by a water single, then have a land double, and usually end with a water double. Pigeons were normally used in the land tests, but because they became quite scarce and because their uneven flight pattern makes them difficult to shoot, many clubs now use shot pheasants instead. In the water tests most clubs use shackled ducks, which means that the wings and feet of the duck are tied, and they are thrown into the water, which does not hurt them. Ducks also are scarce today, so shot ducks are a rarity.

Because of the greatly increased number of Field Trials, with large entries, many judges felt that they did not have time to put on single marks, and often started out with doubles. Also, where marks used to fall a reasonable distance of sixty or seventy yards, now the dogs must be trained to make much longer retrieves, and one hundred yards is not uncommon in the later tests. It is becoming ridiculous, as often the guns are so far away that the handlers have to point them out to their dogs.

In addition to this, the Derby dogs are now being given "right-angle" falls. The well-trained Derby dog of today has to learn a sophisticated bag of tricks to win or place. It is no longer the natural ability and marking of the dogs that is being tested.

David Elliott, a famous old Scottish trainer and one of the first to succeed in the early eastern Field Trials, commented that we have become "idiotically obsessed" with the idea of cramming a year's training into a few months. He feels we consequently ruin, and have to discard, many good dogs that if given a longer time to learn would do very well.

My personal feeling is that most Chesapeakes mature much later than Labradors, and they should be taken along slowly while they are young.

The book says, about Derby dogs, that speed, style and class, as well as outstanding marking ability, are what the judges are supposed to look for and appreciate. It also says that Derby dogs should ideally have a fast departure, on land or into the water. They should make an aggressive search for the fall, have a prompt pick up and have a reasonably fast

Dual Ch. & AFC Tiger's Cub, CD, bred, owned and handled by Eloise Heller. He was trained in the field by Rex Carr and in Obedience by Doug Bundock. Cub won 29 Open and 85½ Amateur licensed Field Trial points—a total of 114½, a record second only to that of his sire, Dual Ch. & AFC Baron's Tule Tiger, CD.

Dual Ch. & AFC Koolwaters' Colt of Tricrown, owned by Michael Paterno.

return. They are supposed to eagerly come to the line, with an obedient attitude. They must have a "good nose," and they are supposed to persevere in their hunt for the bird.

WHERE TO TRAIN

Not everyone has experienced people with whom to train. Your best bet is to attend a picnic trial, or practice session held by the Retriever Club in your area. It is essential that you have someone else throw for you, because otherwise your dog will only go out the distance you can throw. At these training sessions you will meet other people who are interested in training their dogs, so you can work together.

The American Chesapeake Club Regional Director in your area will be very helpful and informative. Try to attend any local Chesapeake Days that are held, and try to get to know other Chesapeake owners who are also interested in Field Trials.

Dual Ch. Cub's Kobi King. Charles Sambrailo purchased him from original owner Helen Hartley. Sambrailo ran him in quite a few trials and took him duck hunting. Kobi made his bench title at age 10½.

Ch. Caroway's Wild Goose Chase, up-and-coming young dog, bred by Carol Andersen and owned by veteran field trialer Roger Reopelle. He amassed 21 Derby points and became a qualified all-age dog when 26 months old.

QUALIFYING STAKE

The next stake for you, after your dog has become two years old and is no longer permitted to run in the Derby, is the Qualifying. The little book says, ''A Qualifying Stake at a Retriever Trial shall be for dogs which have never won first, second, third or fourth place or a Judges'

Dual Ch. & AFC Capital City Jake. "Cappy" was purchased from Eloise Cherry by Jane Kelso Dahl who brought him to the completion of all his titles.

Award of Merit in an Open All-Age, or won first, second, third or fourth place in an Amateur All-Age Stake, or won two first places in Qualifying Stakes.'' In other words, this is an intermediate stake, where the dogs who are just starting their advanced work can compete with each other.

Many Field Trial judges feel that the Qualifying Stake is the hardest to judge. Until the judges run a couple of tests, they cannot tell whether this group of dogs is just out of the Derby or if they are pretty experienced. You, as a handler, will have no way of knowing until the stake starts how hard the tests will be. But you will know that, in addition to being steady to shot, your dog will have to ''Honor.'' This means that after the dog

Dual Ch. Fireweed's Jasmine, bred by Linda Harger and owned by Carol Andersen. "Jazz" is the first Dual Champion Chesapeake bitch.

has had a turn retrieving a bird, that dog will be expected to sit quietly next to you and watch the *other* dog on line with you be sent for a bird.

Qualifying dogs are supposed to be able to mark triple falls. They also are supposed to be able to do simple "blind retrieves," often a hundred yards long.

In a blind retrieve, the dog handlers are called up to stand next to the judges, which is the starting point. From there you are allowed to watch where the bird is placed. The dog has *not* seen this plant. When you run, you are supposed to tell your dog "Get Back," and the dog is supposed to run into the field on the line you gave and look for the bird. If your dog's direction deviates from the original one you gave, you are allowed to blow your whistle. When you do this your dog is supposed to stop, sit, look at you and then take the direction you give with a hand

Dual Ch. & AFC J.J.'s Jessie, CD. Bred by Carol Andersen and owned by Linda Patterson and Jennifer Jaynes.

signal. It really is simpler than it sounds, but you certainly will either have to have a trainer start your dog on this, or train with some knowledgeable people to understand how to do it.

Your dog must be trained to do "triples" on both land and in water. In other words, he must remember each of three fallen birds which have been shot and thrown by three separate gunners.

Until recently, the Qualifying Stake's first test was always a "double" land mark. Then you would be expected to do a "land blind." Normally the field would then move to water and you would have a "water triple." Most Qualifying Stakes used to end with a "water blind."

Like all the other stakes held today there are really too many dogs entered to have enough time to adequately test the ability of the participating dogs. So the tests have become more complicated, which in my opinion is a shame. Few judges of today will start with a mere double on land. What is more usual now is to commence with a single, combined with a blind. Obviously, unless your dog has been taught not to return to the former mark, you are in trouble. It takes a long time to teach a young

Dual Ch. Coot's Gypsy Clipper. Clipper was bred by Carol Andersen and raised and started by Harry Cody. Clipper had all-breed Open placements at 2½-years-old, and since then he has been owned by Dr. Tom Ivey. He has run two Open Nationals and is a deadly marker on land and water.

dog all these new things. It is usually a year or more after they are out of the derby before they can successfully place in a Qualifying.

It is absolutely essential that the dogs be trained with other people and other dogs. Practically no one has successfully trained a Qualifying winner by working alone.

Another important factor is having several different kinds of places to train. On land, you need some green fields, some rice checks, some hilly country, as well as some land that is bisected by creeks. Do not think you can always work on the same pond, or the same kind of pond. You will find, as you attend various Trials in different areas, that some lakes are fringed with heavy tules. Other water tests are held through a series of ponds. Some ponds have islands and peninsulas. A dog who has not been shown these different types of water may well become confused.

AMATEUR ALL-AGE AND OPEN ALL-AGE

The American Kennel Club booklet states that "An Open Age Stake at a Retriever Trial shall be for all dogs." It also says that "An Amateur All-Age Stake at a Retriever Trial shall be for any dogs, if handled in that stake by persons who are Amateurs."

Both the Open and the Amateur Stakes carry points toward a dog's attaining a Field Championship or Amateur Field Championship.

Usually the tests are the same for both of these events. The Open is considered harder to win because you are competing with professional handlers and their expertise. Also, many of the top "pro" handlers will enter five or six dogs, so that gives them a numerical edge over the average amateur with only one dog to run.

However, an astute and dedicated amateur handler, with one well-trained dog, often can and does win the Open All-Age Stake. The one-dog owner is particularly successful in establishing complete rapport with a dog and can give two or three times the amount of work that the professional can give each dog.

Because the dogs are so versatile today, and so well trained on a variety of marking and handling tests, it is necessary to have extremely demanding series to separate the field.

A dog who is fast, stylish, a good marker and in addition wants to please is always a threat in any company. There are some special amateurs—hardworking, competent and with a lot of time in which to train—who can hold their own against any professional. Some of these amateurs even win Open Nationals.

Brosand's Whitefooted Apache, bred, owned and handled by Dr. G. M. Miller. "Pache" finished his Field Trial career at the age of nine, with a remarkable record of placing consistently in Specialty and all-breed Trials, lacking only an all-breed win that would have titled him.

There is no pattern or ruling as to what the tests will be. Normally, the judges start on land, because when they have a large number of dogs to run, land tests go faster than water tests. But All-Age dogs are expected to do triples on land and on water. Sometimes they are even given quadruples on water. They are expected to do not only single blind retrieves, but also double blinds. And a combination of these tests can be given them in any order that the officiating judges wish.

If the stake starts early in the morning, the first test could be a triple mark on land, combined with a double blind retrieve. This would count as two series, after which the dogs that had performed properly would be "Called Back," or invited, to do the next test. The dogs who had poor work would be eliminated from further competition.

You can teach your dog to do blind retrieves when you and the dog are alone. But you will also have to school in doing blinds with a combination of marks, so you will need to have gunners that will shoot birds and then stand still in the field. Your dog may be asked to do blinds that are planted past the gunners, to one side of them, or even through two sets of them, to a spot that is further out.

Ch. Widgeon's Bedazzlin Sunshine, owned by Maggie Hoagland, with challenge trophies won at Chesapeake Specialty and West Coast Trials in 1988.

The titles of Field Champion and Amateur Field Champion are not lightly won. They are attained by a point system, and no points are earned unless there are twelve qualified ''Point'' dogs in the stake.

I have a great admiration for the Obedience dogs who have earned their Utility title. But training for that is simple compared to training for Field Trials. True, the Utility dog works on hand signals. But these are given in an enclosed ring, at a fairly short distance from the handler. In trials, the dogs are often two hundred yards out. When the handler blows the whistle, the dog must stop, respond to an arm signal and be completely under control. It really is quite exciting to watch.

Some of the field tests are called ''Courage'' tests, where the dogs have to go through very tough cover, like nettles or heavy tules. Some dogs will hesitate before entering these obstacles, and will receive a lower score than those who courageously plunge in and through.

Besides the trials held by the various Field Trial clubs in all parts of the country, once a year there are two national events.

The National Retriever Club, usually in November, holds its National Championship Stakes of that year. You have to win an Open Stake, plus two additional Open points to qualify to run. Here professional and amateurs both compete, and the finest dogs of the country run against each other. It is well worth your time to watch this event if it is held in your area.

The National Amateur Retriever Club also holds a National Amateur Championship Stake each year, usually in June. Here, only amateur handlers may compete. To participate you must qualify by winning an Open or an Amateur first place, as well as two additional points. The winner of this event is known as the National Amateur Champion of that year, which, of course, is a big honor.

The entries in both of these national stakes are now uncomfortably large, and the judges are hard pressed to properly test such enormous fields in the four days allotted to the events. Every year some of our Chesapeakes qualify for both of these nationals. Obviously, our breed is greatly outnumbered. But, percentage wise, Chesapeakes are winning more than their share of Field Trial awards.

If you have a good dog, lots of time to train and travel, you will enjoy running in Field Trials. I can't think of a hobby that is more fun.

STATISTICALLY SPEAKING
BY JANET HORN

In 1992, 225 all-breed retriever trials were held, a substantial increase over the 169 reported for 1978. Since the AKC has recognized new retriever clubs and permitted them to hold these additional trials, providing many more opportunities to those who participate in running dogs, it has been suggested that there is a decrease in pressure, reducing the "rat race" deplored by Eloise Cherry and others in the 1970s. In 1978, 29,014 retrievers competed in the four stakes. In 1992, the total number of competing dogs had risen to 32,975. However these figures may balance, anyone who has been in dogs long enough knows that whatever the form of competition, it never gets easier, and in American events the demand for increased expertise in training and handling accompanies the desire for better dogs. Field Trial judges devise ever more difficult tests, and the trainers respond by bringing dogs with the increasingly uncanny ability to perform these tests.

Field Trials will always have devotees in the Chesapeake fancy. As these trials become more esoteric, the Hunting Retriever Tests offer broad opportunities to the many who prefer to excel in hunting; in 1992, 202 Hunting Retriever Tests were held, with a total of 16,188 dogs participating. If we attempt to compare with the number competing in Field Trials, we must remember that entries in the Hunting Tests are limited, and that many will not continue to enter at a given level after they have achieved the title that level confers.

In both Field Trials and Hunting Tests, the Labradors outnumber the other retriever breeds by far, and in 1992 the Labrador Retriever topped all breeds with its registration of 120,879. The Golden Retriever registered 69,850, and the Chesapeake registration was 5,295 in 1992. Percentage-wise, the Chesapeake Bay Retriever more than holds its own in all-retriever Performance Events.

Ch. Ironwood's Stone E. Cubs was Eloise Cherry's last Field Trial contender. After her death "Stoney" was purchased by Dr. Marston Jones, who finished his Canadian Field Trial Championship.

13

Chesapeake Field Trial History and Records

THE COVETED TITLE of Field Champion or Amateur Field Champion is not easily won. Probably, in all breeds, approximately one out of every fifty good Derby dogs are promising enough to go on and be trained for Open and Amateur stakes. Then, alas, many of them prove to be only mediocre in their advanced work.

Behind each dog who wins a Field Trial Championship, or Amateur Field Trial Championship, are many arduous hours of training. To please the judges a dog must be eager, stylish, fast and be an intelligent and willing worker. Outstanding marking ability is required to remember the fall of three, and sometimes four, birds that are shot in the big stakes. Trainability is a definite requisite in learning to do land or water blinds (where birds are hidden, and where the dog is directed to the location of it by his handler). These birds may be planted two hundred yards away from the handler and starting point, and all the handler is permitted to do is to blow a whistle and give the dog arm signals. Absolute control is needed for a good performance, which when it occurs, is thrilling to watch.

In each stake only four places carrying championship points are awarded. The best Labradors and Goldens in the country run in Field Trials, so the Chesapeake is required to defeat other breeds as well. In addition, today's entries are larger than they have ever been.

Relatively few Chesapeakes are run in Field Trials, and we constitute a very small percentage of the all-breed entry. But, fortunately, we have a high percentage of success. It is with pride and pleasure that I give a roster of the Chesapeakes who have made our modern Field Trial history.

CHESAPEAKE DUAL CHAMPIONS

		BREEDER	OWNER
1937	SODAK'S GYPSY PRINCE	Fr. Shuster	A. A. Bliss
	(Bandy Lindy ex Makota's Gypsy Queen)		
1959	MOUNT JOY'S MALLARD	Mt. Joy Kennels	E. C. Fleischmann
	(Nelgard's King Tut ex Sasnakra Sassy)		

FC/AFC Bay City Jake, owned by Dr. Miles Thomas and Peter van der Meulen.

Three generations of Field Champion bitches. Left to Right: FC/AFC J.J.'s Chi-Town Blizzard, Dual Ch. & AFC J.J.'s Jessie, CD, and Dual Ch. Fireweed's Jasmine.

		BREEDER	OWNER
1965	BARON'S TULE TIGER	Eloise Heller	Eloise Heller
	(Nelgard's Baron ex Joanie Teal)		
1965	MEG'S O'TIMOTHY	Quincy Hunt	Dr. F. A. Dashnaw
	(Beewacker's Chester ex Meg O' My Heart)		
1970	KOOLWATERS' COLT OF TRICROWN	Margaret Long	Michael Paterno
	(Bomarc of South Bay ex Welcome of the Willows)		
1970	TIGER'S CUB	Eloise Heller	Eloise Heller
	(Baron's Tule Tiger ex Napolitano's Ladybug)		
1978	CUB'S KOBI KING	Eloise Heller	Charles Sambrailo
	(Tiger's Cub ex Chesa Reid April Echo)		
1981	CAPITAL CITY JAKE	J. & R. Orchard	Jane Kelso
	(Bay City Jake ex Tawny Bri)		
1982	FIREWEED'S JASMINE	Linda Harger	Carol Andersen
	(Aleutian Surf Breaker ex Wildwood's Fireweed)		

133

FC Fireweed's Aleutian Widgeon, bred and owned by Linda Harger.

		BREEDER	OWNER
1987	J. J.'S JESSIE	Carol Andersen	Linda Patterson

(Chesdel Chippewa Chief ex Fireweed's Jasmine)

| 1990 | COOT'S GYPSY CLIPPER | Carol Andersen | Dr. Tom Ivey |

(Captain Cody's Coot Catcher ex Chip's Gypsy of Caroway)

FIELD TRIAL CHAMPIONS FROM 1980

1980   CAPITAL CITY JAKE   Jane Kelso Dahl
(AFC Bay City Jake ex Tawny Bri)

FC CC's Diamond Dex, owned by Christopher Corcoran.

1980 FIREWEED'S   Linda Harger
      ALEUTIAN
      WIDGEON
      (FC/AFC Aleutian Surf Breaker ex Ch. Wildwood's Fireweed)
1981 ROCK HONEYBEAR   James Mauney
      OF THE YUKON
      (FC/AFC/CFTC Chesdel Chippewa Chief ex Oak Hill Raindrop)
1982 ELIJAH'S SUNSHINE   Steve & Sharon Parker
      SALLY
      (Jake's Elijah ex Wally's Teton Sunshine)
1985 CH. FIREWEED'S   Carol Andersen
      JASMINE
      (FC/AFC Aleutian Surf Breaker ex Ch. Wildwood's Fireweed)

AFC Arctic Sunshine Sally, owned by Bill Burks and Steve Parker.

1987 S. & S.'S SUNSHINE   Steve & Sharon Parker
       MEG
       (FC/AFC Aleutian Surf Breaker ex FC/AFC Elijah's Sunshine
       Sally)
1987 J.J.'S JESSIE   Jennifer Jaynes and Linda Patterson
       (FC/AFC/CFTC/CAFTC Chesdel Chippewa Chief ex Dual Ch.
       Fireweed's Jasmine)
1989 COOT'S GYPSY   Tom & Marianne Ivey
       CLIPPER
       (Captain Cody's Coot Catcher ex Chip's Gypsy of Caroway)

136

AFC Stoney's Way To Go Harry, owned and handled by Dr. Marston Jones.

1991 J.J.'S CHI-TOWN   J. M. & L. S. Patterson
        BLIZZARD
     (Humboldt Bay Skipper, MH, ex Dual Ch. AFC J.J.'s Jessie)
1991 CC'S DIAMOND DEX   Christopher Corcoran
     (Berteleda's Baron of Caroway ex Chip's Sweet Sassy Sheila)
1992 ED'S TURNPIKE   Edward & Lottie Shetzler
        DRIFTER
     (Piney Neck's Deacon ex Kirby's Keeper)

AMATEUR FIELD TRIAL CHAMPIONS FROM 1980

1980 CAPITAL CITY JAKE   Jane Kelso
     (AFC Bay City Jake ex Tawny Bri)
1981 ROCK HONEYBEAR   James Mauney
        OF THE YUKON
     (FC/AFC/CFTC Chesdel Chippewa Chief ex Oak Hill Raindrop)
1982 ELIJAH'S SUNSHINE   Steve & Sharon Parker
        SALLY
     (Jake's Elijah ex Wally's Teton Sunshine)
1984 S. & S.'S SUNSHINE   Steve & Sharon Parker
        MEG
     (FC/AFC Aleutian Surf Breaker ex FC/AFC Elijah's Sunshine
        Sally)

AFC Foxridge's Riddley Walker, bred by Shirli Hayes, owned and handled by Brett Crow. "Pike" is a large dark brown dog of good conformation and excellent disposition.

FC/AFC Elijah's Sunshine Sally, owned by Steve and Sharon Parker, with her sire, Ch. Jake's Elijah, and daughter FC/AFC S. & S.'s Sunshine Meg.

1988 J.J.'S JESSIE   Jennifer Jaynes and Linda Patterson
     (FC/AFC/CFTC/CAFTC Chesdel Chippewa Chief ex Dual Ch.
        Fireweed's Jasmine)
1989 DELAWARE CITY   Lottie Shetzler
        LADY
     (Burning Tree's Outer Banks ex Taffy's Honey)
1990 FOXRIDGE'S   Brett Crow
        RIDDLEY WALKER
     (Tiger's Atom Kodiak ex Whiskey's Lady)
1991 J.J.'S CHI-TOWN   J. M. & L. S. Patterson
        BLIZZARD
     (Humboldt Bay Skipper, MH, ex Dual Ch. AFC J.J.'s Jessie)
1992 ED'S TURNPIKE   Edward & Lottie Shetzler
        DRIFTER
     (Piney Neck's Deacon ex Kirby's Keeper)
1992 STONEY'S WAY TO   Dr. Marston Jones
        GO HARRY
     (CFTC/CAFTC Ironwood's Stone E Cubs ex Ch. Berteleda's
        Ready or Not)

Ch. Willowpond T G I F, CD, WD, a multiple Sporting Group winner and the sire of 24 Champions. Breeders-owners-handlers throughout his career: Edith and Doug Hanson.

14

Showing the Chesapeake Bay Retriever

by Nat Horn

THE INTENDED AUDIENCE of this book includes people who know little or nothing about dog shows, those who have a limited knowledge of dog shows and those who have shown their Chesapeakes over a significant amount of time. This topic is divided into parts: the beginner, the breeder / owner / handler, the advanced competition exhibitor and conditioning and preparation. This chapter is devoted to those who wish to show their own dog. I will not enter into a detailed discussion about the selection of professional handlers. If you do go this avenue, please take the time to understand the difference between the true professional and the agent who collects a fee and calls himself or herself a professional.

THE BEGINNER

If you haven't been to a dog show, you should attend several of these events and spectate. Learn how the classes are organized, how a championship is achieved and the nature of the advanced competition. Once you have done this, it is advisable to find out how your dog will fare in competition. Sometimes this is difficult. *Read the breed Standard,* observe what happens and talk to knowledgeable people about Chesapeakes and dogs in general.

In addition to having a dog that can win, you will need to possess the ability to present your dog well. This comes with time and experience. A good way to learn is to attend handling seminars offered by top professional handlers. It is usually not advisable to take your instructions from someone who has just a little more experience than yourself. This person may teach you things that develop into bad handling habits. There are also good books available written by top professional handlers. You will learn to pose your dog properly, to move your dog in a trot *and* to grin and bear it when things don't go well. *Good sportsmanship is a must.* One thing that I must stress, dog showing should be an extremely happy experience for your dog and you. It is important to remember *it is a hobby.*

THE BREEDER/OWNER/HANDLER

There are a large number of Chesapeake owners who fall into this category. They have completed several championships, breed puppies

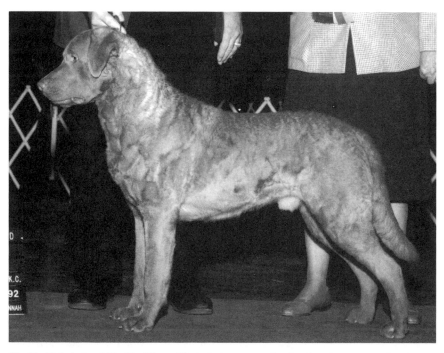

Ch. Parklake's Lordship Sir Oliver, titled at eleven months, bred and owned by Carole and Jim Bomberger and handled by Jim.

periodically and continue to finish dogs that they own as well as dogs that they have bred. Most of these people are dedicated to their breed, love Chesapeakes and enjoy getting out to the shows. They also do many other things with their dogs, e.g., Obedience, field work and just plain enjoying their family pet.

Some of these exhibitors show their dogs extremely well; some of these exhibitors have better dogs than others. It is extremely helpful to continue to attend the advanced seminars held by top professional handlers. Even the experts will tell you, you never know it all. You can always learn new techniques and improve your abilities. To qualify successfully for the higher levels of competition, one needs a near-great dog. In addition to this, your handling skills must be excellent. A great deal of time, dedication, hard work and stamina are required on the part of the exhibitor.

RING KNOW-HOW FOR THE NOVICE

Showing your dog can be fun for both you and your dog. You should begin by attending a show or a match and observing what will be expected of you and your dog. Match shows are informal, comparatively inexpensive, and their purpose is to provide experience for novice handlers, inexperienced dogs and aspirant judges. In the conformation ring dogs are judged on type, conformation to the Standard, soundness, condition, temperament and breed character. For a judge to properly and accurately evaluate all these different things in only the few minutes alloted by the AKC, the handler must present the dog well. The judge needs to see the dog standing still, gaiting smoothly, and must be able to completely examine the dog with his/her hands.

To present the dog in a "show pose," it is necessary to learn to "set up" or "stack" the dog. Some dogs naturally set themselves up very nicely, but they must all learn to let themselves be positioned as the handler wishes and to hold the pose. Before you set the dog up, walk your dog around a bit on lead, then stop in a standing position with your right hand in front of the dog's face, as in a Stay signal. With a dog who has been trained to sit, you may need to reach quickly back to place your left hand in front of the dog's stifles (knees).

Place the forelegs, left leg first, so that they are perpendicular from the elbow to the ground, and absolutely parallel with feet the same distance apart as the elbows. Feet should point straight ahead, not toeing out or in. Place one foreleg at a time by grasping the elbow, lifting and turning the leg and foot until they are straight. Make front leg adjustments

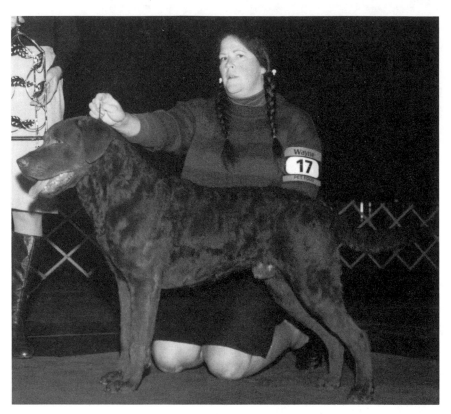

Ch. Redlion's Bear of Upper Creek, WDX, bred, owned and handled by Jane Pappler. Bear was the only Group I winning Chesapeake with licensed Field Trial awards.

by grasping the elbow; never try to place a foot by holding the foot or the pastern. When the dog's front is properly supported, the forelegs are perpendicular from the elbow to the ground, and the elbow is directly underneath the withers (shoulders). The greater part of the dog's weight is supported in front; however, this is a four-legged animal, and is in equilibrium only when each leg takes its fair share of weight.

Set the rear legs, left leg first, one at a time, with the rear toes pointing straight ahead and the hocks perpendicular to the ground. The distance between the hocks should be about the same as the width of the chest. The rear leg in profile should show a good bend of stifle; some dogs have more and some have less, so the essential point here is to keep the hock straight, vertical and perpendicular to the ground. Looked at from the rear, the hocks should be parallel, turning neither in nor out. Do not try to place a hind leg by grasping the foot. In placing a foot, front or rear, always lift the leg and place it where you want it.

Ch. Chestnuthills Pandora, CDX, owned by Karen and Ronald Anderson, placed in the Group under William L. Kendrick, handled by Karen who also trained and handled her in Obedience.

After the rear is set up, check the front and make any adjustments if necessary. When the rear is set, gently float the tail out behind the dog by running your left hand under the tail, which should never be tucked between the hind legs. A wagging tail or a naturally good tail carriage is best left alone and the dog may be held only by the head. It is equally acceptable to hold the posed dog by both head and tail. You can practice in front of a large mirror to see your dog set up just as a judge would see it.

IN THE RING

The first thing on entering the show ring is to walk to the designated spot and set the dog up while waiting for the rest of the class or for the judging to begin.

In examining a dog, the judge begins with the head. Until you and your dog are very well schooled, always keep a hand on your dog so that the dog knows you are still there. The judge must examine the dog's bite; that is, the way the front teeth meet. Some prefer to ask the handler to show the bite, so be prepared to hold your dog's teeth closed while lifting the lips and holding the head so the judge may see the bite.

In examining a male, a judge is required to check for the presence of ''two normal testicles normally descended into the scrotum.'' Females

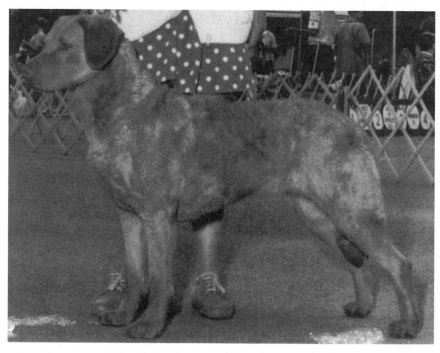

Ch. Willowpond Chesany Duchess, bred by Jan Holshevnikoff and owned by Robbin Phillips and Edith Hanson. Owner-handled to a record number of Sporting Group placements for a Chesapeake bitch.

have no corresponding ordeal; however, it is as well to bear in mind that a bitch coming in season is often more touchy than usual around the hindquarters.

When the judge is examining all dogs in turn before gaiting them, keep your dog posed until the judge has gone over the following dog in line. Some judges like to look back at the preceding dog to make a comparison before going on. In a large class you may then relax your dog, but keep track, and as the judge is going over the last dog, start to set your dog up in the show position. If individual gaiting immediately follows examination, then set up your dog for the judge's final look at the class as the last dog is gaiting.

Gaiting

Dogs are gaited at a trot because this is the gait that best reveals their structure. Viewed in profile, it shows reach and drive; soundness is assessed from the view coming and going. Since dogs are expected to move around the ring in a counterclockwise direction, and to be shown from the left side of the handler, always hold the lead in your left hand only, leaving the right hand free.

When gaiting, hold your leash hand far enough out from your body to keep daylight between you and the dog, so that the judge can see everything about the dog being moved. Practice gaiting and find the speed at which your dog naturally moves best and adjust your own gait accordingly. Teach yourself to take long strides and "move out." Beginners almost always try to trip along with mincing little steps, and your dog will try to move this way too, if this is what you do. You don't want your dog trying to hold back; you want the dog to move out with enthusiasm, so you must learn to do this too.

A dog that is properly put together looks best gaited on a loose lead, and the beginner should learn to use the lead so the dog will learn to trust the lead and to respond to it. These results cannot be obtained by stringing up and holding the dog that way. A series of quick jerks is preferable to a long steady pull that may cause a dog to balk or pull the other way. The dog should not be forced, but rather encouraged, and corrections must always be followed with praise.

When a dog's head drops while gaiting, reach over with your right hand and give a chuck under the chin, saying "Head up," or something of the sort. A dog can learn to gait with the head up, if you teach this. If you then use a tight lead, your Chesapeake will gait head up and won't take the attitude that this is torture.

Gaiting away from the judge, take your first few steps at a walk, and build up to the speed at which your dog trots best. When coming back, slow down gradually as you come to a stop about six feet from the judge, and watch so you can walk your dog into naturally standing true when stopped.

Listen carefully to the judge's instructions, and if you do not understand, you may ask for repetition. Try to do exactly as you are asked, and don't add your own embellishments. "Straight down and back" means straight, so you must learn to chart your course and stay on it. Indoors you may be able to follow a strip of matting; be sure you keep your dog on the mat, which is there to provide sure footing. Outdoors, choose an object on the horizon—a ring marker, a tree or whatever, and aim your dog straight for it. When you make the about turn, look up to see where the judge is, and coming back keep the dog aimed straight for the judge. As the dog is presented to the judge at the end of the gaiting, expression and appearance of alertness are an essential part of the presentation. Use your right hand to offer a toy or a tidbit held fairly high so

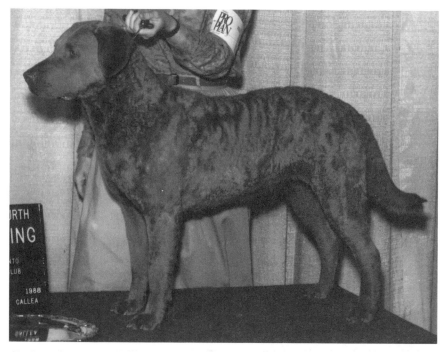

Ch. Frost Hill's Diana, WD, bred by Cathy Azevedo, owned by Kathy and Phil McKibbin and always handled by Kathy.

Ch. Snocree's Golden Beast of R.C., CD, owner-handler Kathy Mines Rayner. Elsa was Rocky Creek Kennels' foundation bitch jointly owned by the Mines sisters, Kathy, and Janice Mines Bykowsky. Elsa earned a CD at age ten.

your dog's head will be raised with ears up and an alert, interested expression. Some judges like to elicit the dog's reaction by making little noises and offering their own tidbits, so you should be ready for this, too.

When I say "aim your dog," I mean exactly that. A dog must move in the direction the spine is pointed, so as you move, make sure the dog's body is in a straight line in the direction you want to go. If the dog is not straight, a quick, light jerk should remedy the situation.

The thing to keep in mind is that the judge has to be able to see the dog in order to judge the dog. You have brought the dog to show to the judge, and you must learn to handle so as not to conceal any part of the dog with your hands and arms and to avoid placing your body between the dog and the judge. Beyond this, keep *your* attention on the judge. Make sure a judge sees what he/she wants to see now, and learn to anticipate what will be wanted next. Little or no conversation takes place in the ring. Most match-show judges are sympathetic to the beginner, patient and helpful, and thoughtfully approach the puppy or inexperienced dog to help make the show a pleasant experience. Most point-show judges

Am. & Can. Ch. Eastern Waters' Break O'Day, Am/Can CD, JH, WD, bred and owned by
Janet Horn. Dan Horn handled "Breakers" in the shows while Janet trained and handled him
in Obedience and in the field. Breakers was Best of Breed in the ACC Specialty Show 1987,
and received a Judge's Award of Merit in 1986 and 1989. His 104 Bests of Breed included
three ACC Supported Entry shows, and BOB at Westminster Kennel Club 1984. He had 19
Sporting Group placements.

are sympathetic and helpful as far as the very strict time schedule prescribed by the AKC permits, but they have very little time for the novice
handler and the unschooled dog.

Showing dogs is considered to be a sport for ladies and gentlemen,
and good manners and deportment are supported by a dress code that is
observed by handlers and judges. A prominent professional handler says,
"Getting ready to show a dog, you should dress as if you are going to
do something important." A sport jacket is appropriate for a man, with
a shirt and tie, and the jacket is kept on in the ring except in the hottest
weather. If a male judge chooses to remove his jacket, handlers may feel
free to do the same. Ladies wear skirts, dresses or a neat, well-tailored
pants suit. "Split skirts" are seen, but however feminine fashions change

and skirt lengths fluctuate, simple, uncluttered clothing styled to permit graceful and free movement is always appropriate. At least one pocket is essential to one's ring outfit. Shoes should have flat heels and be comfortable. It is your dog that you are showing, so do not dress to call attention to yourself. Avoid anything conspicuous or bizarre. Find a comfortable, well-made outfit, put it on and forget about it.

While teaching yourself and your dog the basics of ring deportment, you will be developing the style and showmanship that are essential to a competitive performance. Keeping your dog happy in this teamwork will bring enhancement to your relationship. Showing your dog should be a happy activity for both of you. The underlying principle of good handling, whether in show, field or Obedience, is always, to borrow words spoken by Wilson Davis many years ago, "Make it look as good as you can." For further information, write the American Kennel Club, 51 Madison Avenue, New York, N.Y. 10010, and request the booklet *Rules Applying to Registration and Dog Shows* for definitive information on classes, awards, eligibilities, etc., as prescribed in the official structure of the sport.

ADVANCED COMPETITION

Relatively few Chesapeake exhibitors participate at this level. Typically, there are breeds that do well in the Sporting group. The Golden, the Springer Spaniel, the Pointer and the Irish Setter, to name a few. Breeds like the Chesapeake, Flat-Coated Retriever, Field Spaniel and German Wirehaired Pointer only do well when a very special dog emerges and someone is willing to put great effort behind it.

This is an area that fascinates me. At the Group and Best in Show level, there are four needed ingredients to success: a dog of great quality, superior handling presentation, financial resources and commitment that requires devoting a great deal of time and hard work to the effort.

Getting that great dog! No matter how you got it; bought it, bred it or if somebody gave it to you, you've got to have a sound dog. A dog that moves well coming toward you, going away from you and from the side. As you start competing in the Group, sound movement gets weighed more and more. Your dog is being compared against other breeds, not just other Chesapeakes. You really get a strong message on how judges can differ regarding the Chesapeake when it comes to Group judging:

- Some never place a Chesapeake in the Group.
- Some will place a Chesapeake when they feel they can because they like the breed.

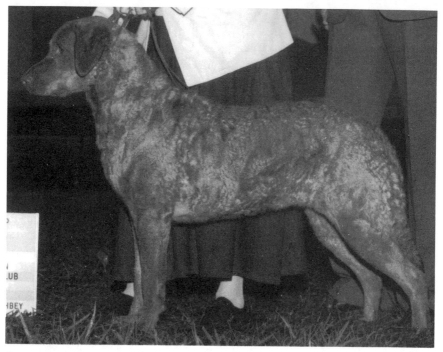

Ch. Eastern Waters' Keep the Dream, the only Chesapeake bitch to win multiple Sporting Group Firsts. "Keeper," bred, owned and handled by Janet Horn, had to the end of 1992 45 Bests of Breed and six Group placements.

- Some treat all breeds equally and, if deserving, the Chesapeake gets a placement.
- Some judges like to place one of the breeds third or fourth in the Group that normally don't place.
- Some judges like to place a Pointer, a Spaniel, a Retriever and a Setter. This is known as the "All-Round" method.

There are many factors that are applied in Group judging. Judges are human beings and see things from different perspectives. The point here is you have to know where the judge is coming from. If judge A has not ever placed a Chesapeake in forty years, the chances are you don't want to travel five hours to get into the Group under that person. On the other hand, if a judge has a history of placing top-winning Chesapeakes, this is the direction you want to go in. Another important factor, Groups are often referred to as tough Groups, good Groups and even weak Groups. It becomes very difficult if seven or eight of the dogs in the Group are Best in Show dogs and typically place in most of the Groups

Ch. Chesabar's Sea-J, breeder-owner-handler Patsy Barber. "Bomber" is a multiple Best of Breed and Group winner.

in which they compete. There are other Groups in which judges find themselves struggling to find a fourth place. If you are trying to break in, and the judge likes good Chesapeakes, you sometimes need these medium competitive Groups in which to compete.

One of the things you need to remember is that you are an amateur, competing against professional handlers. You need to show your dog as well as a professional, you need to look the part and you need to accept the fact that they can often outshine you because they have years and years of experience. Don't be discouraged. With hard work and great effort, you will prevail and do your share of winning.

One thing that is important is to realize that breeds stand out for different reasons; for example, glamour goes with the Irish Setter, the Golden Retriever and the American Cocker Spaniel. The Pointer displays impressive nobility. I have found that judges notice Chesapeakes when they show animation, a happy and willing-to-work attitude, charisma and a kind of self-important presence.

GETTING A REPUTATION

The more you and your dog win, the more the dog will be considered by the judges. Judges see Groups, and they see dogs placing, and they see dogs considered. If the dog is pulled out with others and considered for a placement, this is called a "cut."

Judges sometimes talk about the dogs and the different breeds. There are also weekly periodicals in which you can advertise your wins. No one really admits to knowing how much this helps. Judging by the amount of advertising, I would venture to say it doesn't hurt.

CAMPAIGNING

As I stated earlier, a great deal of effort and work, as well as strategy, go into this venture: travel, money (entry fees, motels, gas,

Ch. Homespun's Snooker, bred and handled by Marie Guthier, owned by Barry Gerhart and Marie Guthier. Snooker has multiple Group placements.

154

advertising, etc.) and time and effort. Most of us who are owner-handlers have a full-time job, too. This means when you are not busy with your "other" job, you are eating, breathing and sleeping the efforts to campaign your Chesapeake.

CONDITIONING AND PREPARATION

During the week you must do what is needed to keep your dog in the best condition so that the dog moves as soundly as possible. This requires walking at a trot either on foot, using a bicycle for yourself, or whatever other method you choose to use. Handlers use a mechanical device like a treadmill, called a trotter. Swimming and retrieving on land are also good ways to firm up a dog's muscles. It is important not to overdo it and not to overload a dog with muscle.

Remember a dog is an athlete like a swimmer or a runner, not a

Am. & Can. Ch. Baron of Shorewaters Bussy, with 99 Sporting Group placements including 13 Group I's. Owned by Patsy and Rudy Barber, handler Dennis Kniola.

weightlifter. One of the advantages of showing a Chesapeake is that hours and hours of brushing and trimming are not required. Basically you keep your dog healthy, feed a good food, keep the coat in good condition, trim the toe nails, keep the teeth clean and, if you desire, neaten the whiskers (trimming whiskers is optional).

STRATEGY

Strategy is a great part of the preparation. You must consider your competition, know what the judges look for in a dog and figure out where the competition will go. Sometimes it is best to double enter. You may have a show where you're not too enthused about the breed judge, but you would love to have a shot under the Group judge. Somewhere else the breed judge is great, and the Group judge is just a possibility. When the entries come back and you are the only Special (champion) under that questionable judge, you can go. Still realize that there is no guarantee the judge will not put the class dog over you for Best of Breed.

My point is, there is a lot more to this than going to shows. Good luck to anyone who tries. It is a challenge, and with success, it is very rewarding.

THE CHESAPEAKE IN JUNIOR SHOWMANSHIP
BY SARAH HORN

For Chesapeake fanciers with children, Junior Showmanship can be a rewarding and exciting experience that enables children to become involved in the dog sport with their parents. Entering in Juniors gives the child something to look forward to at the show, a worthwhile hobby on which to focus and valuable experience for later years. Being a Junior handler is a very unique experience.

Showing in Junior Showmanship is quite different from conformation classes. Rather than judging the quality of the dog, the judge considers only the ability of the handler to display and present the dog. To be a Junior handler at an American Kennel Club licensed dog show, Juniors must be between the ages of ten and eighteen. The dog exhibited can be of any breed, but must be owned by the child or a family member.

Classes of Competition

Children between ten and fourteen exhibit in the Novice Junior class and the Open Junior class, while older children between fourteen and

Sarah Horn had many Junior Showmanship wins with Ch. Eastern Waters' Royal Topaz. Topaz was Sarah's housemate through her graduation from college.

eighteen exhibit in the Novice Senior or Open Senior class. Beginning Juniors must exhibit in the Novice class. Upon winning three first places, the Junior then enters the Open class where the serious competition begins. For example, a ten-year-old might show in the Novice Junior class for five to six months before receiving three wins and becoming eligible for Open Junior. Once a Junior has achieved the Open position, he or she does not have to show in a Novice class again. Open Juniors go straight into the Open Senior class on their fourteenth birthday.

Many Juniors practice at matches that allow even younger children to participate in the dog sport. Matches allow eight- nine- and ten-year-old children to practice for the big day at AKC shows. At the first show I entered, I was five years old, showing a dog not only older, but bigger than I was.

Advancing

Once Juniors achieve Open Class status, they compete for two goals. First, Juniors endeavor to win eight first places. If eight firsts are earned, the Junior is entitled to enter the Junior Showmanship competition at the Westminster Kennel Club at Madison Square Garden the following February. Showing at the Garden is a prestigious and great accomplishment. I still remember fondly the exciting feeling of walking into that ring knowing I was with the best Juniors in the country. Other more serious competitors aspire to earn points for their showing ability. In this case, seconds, thirds and fourths are important as well as the coveted firsts. Juniors who receive one of the four places count how many Juniors they defeated on that particular day. Each Junior equals one point. Points then add up each year to show which Juniors are at the top.

Being a Junior Handler with a Chesapeake Bay Retriever has both its advantages and disadvantages. So few Juniors show this breed that a Junior with a Chesapeake will undoubtedly stand out from among those with the many more popular breeds such as a Golden Retriever or Irish Setter. For years I was known as the girl with the Chesapeake, giving me individuality that my friends who showed more popular breeds could not hope to achieve. In addition, Chesapeake Bay Retrievers are incredibly smart, and can be well trained if one works hard.

This intelligence can also be a disadvantage as well. My Juniors dog, Ch. Eastern Waters Royal Topaz, was too intelligent. That is, she easily sensed when I became nervous or tense while preparing for the show. She was so in tune to my emotions that she would also become nervous.

Another disadvantage of showing a Chesapeake Bay Retriever is that many judges simply know nothing about the breed. Junior showmanship is judged by licensed judges of all different breeds, many who have never judged a Sporting dog. Once a judge placed me fourth out of four, and told me that I was in first place until she realized that I had set up Topaz incorrectly. The judge had noticed that although my gaiting patterns were correct, Topaz looked higher in the rear. If the judge had known anything about Chesapeake Bay Retrievers, she would have known this is an acceptable breed characteristic! Once I corrected her on this, there was little hope of having the opportunity to show under her again, because so many judges are eligible to judge Juniors, it is unlikely to show under a particular individual more than once. Considering the challenges of showing a Chesapeake in Juniors, I became even more proud when I was successful. I knew each time I won, that I deserved the win.

Z's Timberwynd placed in the Group under Del Glodowski, from the Open class to Best of Breed over Specials. Owned by Mary Ellen Mazzola, handled by Haley Cullen.

A Valuable Experience

Showing in Junior Showmanship can be a great experience for a child, and instills many qualities and values useful for life. For me, it instilled a great respect, admiration and love for animals, dedication and responsibility, healthy competitiveness and provided many valuable friendships. Most of all, I learned skills for showing dogs at a young age that will last throughout my lifetime. Although I had always loved my dogs, showing them enabled me to see their special loyalty and generosity. Topaz was most patient with me even when we had been in the ring for an hour. Many Junior judges could not decide who to place, and would gait us over and over again and expect us to have the dogs set up on all occasions. I learned to always put the dog's comfort before a win. If it was hot out or if Topaz was tired, there was no way a judge could expect me to put her through all of that again.

I also learned responsibility and dedication. I realized that in order to win, I had to work hard and be dedicated. The most serious Junior might practice every night, whereas other Juniors might practice only before the night of the show, or not at all. The less serious Juniors will do little winning once they are in Open Senior. Competitiveness is extreme in this class, so much so that one professional handler remarked to me that it was worse than Best in Show. However, most Juniors do not allow the competitiveness to come between friendships.

Showing in Junior Showmanship gave me a sense of healthy competition. I realized that you cannot win every time. I learned to be gracious and proud of others who were successful. I also learned how to pick up and try again after a particular bad experience.

In addition, I formed many valuable friendships with other Junior handlers. We never let who won on a particular day affect us. My father often reminds me how it was often impossible to find me between the breed, Juniors and Group judging because I was constantly with my friends.

Junior Showmanship also gave me skills I needed when showing in the conformation classes. After turning seventeen, the cut-off age at that time, I went on to gain a championship on Topaz's son, Ch. Eastern Water's Diamond Dust, and earned his first three Group placements.

15

Chesapeake
Bench History

T HE FIRST American dog show was held in 1874. Sponsored by local organizations, the early dog shows were for exhibition of specimens of the sporting breeds, mostly pointers and setters. The National American Kennel Club was founded in 1876, and its Stud Book registered pointers, setters, spaniels and Chesapeake Bay dogs and retrievers, and there were classes for these breeds in the shows.

The first recorded showing of Chesapeake Bay ducking dogs was at a local event in Baltimore, in connection with the Poultry and Fanciers Association Show in 1877, and here was found the affirmative answer to the question, could the Chesapeake Bay ducking dog be called a breed? The American Kennel Club was founded in 1884, and its Stud Books and show records are a source for breed history, although few Chesapeakes were shown in its first two or three decades.

The first Chesapeake bench champion was Barnum, whelped in 1883, by Monday out of Maryland, bred and owned by G. W. Kierstead. At that time the requirement for championship was three first places, and Barnum won his in 1887, 1891 and 1892, listed each time with different owners. Barnum apparently became well known, for he was the subject of more than one painting by the artist J. M. Tracy, who appears to have specialized in Sporting dogs. Cleveland by Grover Cleveland out of Reta was the second champion, finishing in 1898, owned by B. Alton Smith. The third champion was Deacon, the result of a brother-sister mating by Oak out of Mary, owned by F. C. Fowler.

EARLY SHOWS

The purpose of the early dog shows was the improvement of the breed, and through conformation, the working ability of these Sporting dogs. Later the fancy breeds were included in all-breed shows. The aim of making these breeds known through public exhibitions became more important, as did the competitive spirit that flourishes wherever opportunity appears. The Hursts' Chesacroft Kennels in Maryland began seriously to campaign their dogs in the 1920s and made many champions. The

Ch. Eastern Waters' Oak, CD, TD, WD, winning Best of Breed, ACC Specialty Show 1968 from the classes under the well-known retriever specialist, James A. Cowie. Oak won his second Specialty Best of Breed in 1975 from the Veteran Class. On both occasions he was owner-handled by Rupert Humer. Oak was owned by Rupe and Betsy Humer, and he was Rupe's first hunting dog.

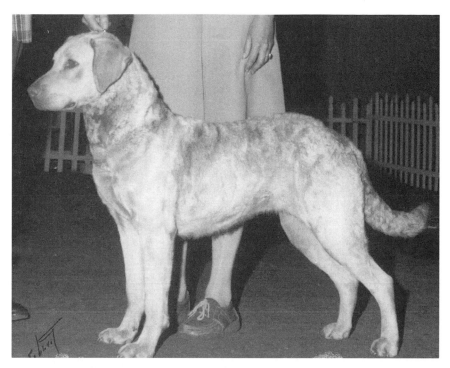

Ch. Stoney Creek Hopscotch, CD, Best of Breed, ACC Specialty 1983 under Sporting specialist Ralph Del Deo. She was owner-handled by Kellie Lewis, and was Snowfield Kennel's foundation bitch.

American Chesapeake Club was active in the Midwest and held a Specialty show in 1926. Best of Breed was one of Matt Barron's several champions, Barron's Lily Pad of the Barron and Orr Kennels. The next Specialty was held in 1933 as the club's headquarters moved to the East, and Best of Breed was Ch. Bud Parker's Ripple, owned by Anthony A. Bliss. Specialty shows were held in successive years after that until the interruption of World War II. In 1946 forces were summoned to hold a Specialty at Devon, Pennsylvania, and Best of Breed was Mrs. A. W. Owens's Ch. Cindy of Greenridge. Interest in showing seemed to have declined, and it was not until 1954 that the ACC held its next Specialty show. Since then the event has been held every year with the exception of 1958.

During the 1950s and 1960s the Chesapeake classes at a selected all-breed show were designated as the ACC Specialty Show. As entries increased and interest grew, we looked forward to holding our Specialty as an independent event, and in 1972 the first separate Specialty since the war took place at Marshy Point, which remains as one of the original old ducking shores on the Chesapeake Bay.

As the National Specialties rotate around the country, they are sometimes independent and other times part of an all-breed show depending on circumstances in the area where the show is held. For a very few years, a second or Regional Specialty was also held by the club, but this scheme was abandoned a number of years ago, while the club sponsors several supported entry shows throughout the year in different parts of the country. These events help to put the breed before the public as well as attracting gatherings of Chesapeake fanciers.

Tony Bliss wrote, as far back as 1936, "We are attempting to encourage the exhibiting of Chesapeakes for the sake of showing the public what our dog looks like and to bring out the great disposition and character, and also to bring breeders together so that a better understanding of the best type of Chesapeake may be arrived at by all fanciers.

"Our whole aim is to make the Chesapeake as popular in the minds of the public and dog show enthusiasts as the more fashionable and stylish terriers and setters. But we do not wish to have the breed become a show dog, known for its looks. We are aiming to make the Chesapeake popular because of his practical value as a retriever, companion or guard." He concluded, "Our ambition is to see the Chesapeake begin to top all other breeds at the important shows and trials throughout the country. But our primary purpose is to promote Field Trials to such an extent as forever to prevent bench shows from fashioning and spoiling the Chesapeake Bay Retriever."

A MORE RECENT VIEW

Eloise Cherry, a more recent Field Trial fancier, wrote: "Bench shows are very important because the awarding of a championship title in almost all instances guarantees a sound dog. It certainly establishes that the dog has no flaws that are considered disqualifications, such as a poor mouth, black color or a curly coat. It means, as well, that the dog is well adjusted and not shy, able to perform in front of a crowd. Permitting the judge to touch and inspect him means that the dog has a friendly nature. He must also behave well in the presence of other dogs, for if he did not, any conscientious judge would dismiss him from the ring for bad conduct.

"We are fortunate, in the Chesapeake breed, that we do not have two distinct types—a show dog and a working dog. . . . They give one a sense of their strength and power, and the impression of a dog who can do the work it was intended to do.''

TODAY'S SHOWS

The nature of Field Trials limits participation, and we now have more ''show people'' in Chesapeakes than ever before. From the 1930s on, the idea of having a title at each end of a dog's name became increasingly popular, and many champion Chesapeakes also earned Obedience and Tracking titles, giving their owners added satisfaction as well as demonstrating trainability and ability to work.

The American Chesapeake Club Working Certificate was introduced to show that the dog could do what the breed was intended for, and owners who welcomed this as a tool to aid breeding programs went happily on to the hunting retriever tests which are the most recent performance event offered to us by the American Kennel Club. In all of these

Am. & Can. Ch. Redlion's J. J. Sample, Am/Can CD, WD. Best of Breed, ACC Specialty Show, 1979, under Mrs. E. Tipton. "J.J." was bred, owned and handled by Jane Pappler who produced this outstanding dog in her first litter.

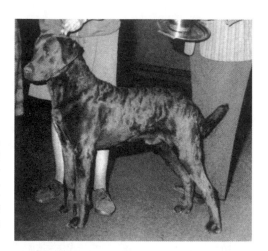

Ch. Teal's Tiger, WD, owned by Susan Steuben and handled by Edith Hanson, was Best in Show at Chintimini Kennel Club (Oregon) in 1978. Teal had 36 Group placements including eight Group I's, and was Best of Breed at the 1977 National Specialty Show.

Am. & Can. Ch. Chesrite's Justin Tyme, CD, WD, Best in Show at Wampanoag Kennel Club in 1979 under Irene Schlintz, breeder-owner-handled by Jan Thomas. Justin's 15 Group placements included three Group I Firsts.

areas of performance an owner can enjoy training and handling the dog, and this is also true of showing a Chesapeake in conformation, for the backbone of the exhibitors in this breed is the breeder-owner-handler who finds showing is another way of enjoying a dog's companionship as well as displaying pride in the dog.

Dog shows are a sport that has many levels, and their complexity has increased over the past fifteen to twenty years. As new exhibitors are assimilated into the fancy, so are new judges. Perhaps especially in the case of the Chesapeake, diversity in breed type sometimes leads to confusion that distorts the overall picture of the breed. Out of this more Chesapeakes are placing in the Sporting Groups than ever before, and the eighteen Best in Show awards won by the breed have all occurred within the last eighteen years. Whether or not the achievement of "show dog" status has affected the Chesapeake Bay Retriever, it remains and is now the only one of the retriever breeds that can, at the present time, produce a dual champion.

BEST IN SHOW CHESAPEAKES

Since they are not considered to be "show dogs," Chesapeakes have often been perceived as lacking "flash," or "glamour," and for many years it was only in exceptional circumstances that one placed in the Sporting Group. As exhibitors demonstrated more interest in this form of all-breed competition, the increase in frequency of Group awards proved this breed to be deserving, yet it took fifty years after a Chesapeake won first in Group for the first time before the breakthrough that brought to the breed its first Best in Show. From 1975 through 1992, fifteen Chesapeakes won all-breed Bests in Show, two of them winning it more than once. Half were owner-handled, the rest presented by professionals. The owner who consistently succeeds in competition with professionals strives to equal the "pros" in expertise, and welcomes the challenge of the campaign. It is with great pride that the Best in Show Chesapeakes are presented:

1975   CH. CRISPIN RODERICK, CD   John & Karen Ann Wood
       (Wabash Country Jake ex Chapel Jene, CD)
1975   AM. & CAN. CH. POND VIEW   W. C. & Ruthann Eller
       BOLT, CD, WD
       (Ch. Breakwater Dirk of Quickstep, CD, WD,
         ex Chesarab's Little Kara)

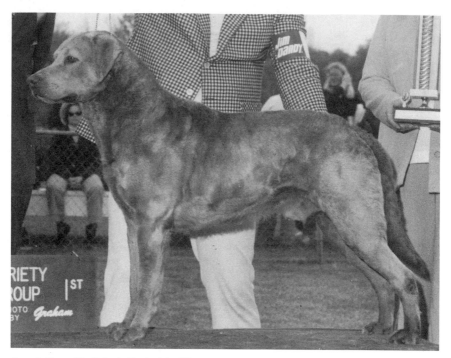

Am. & Can. Ch. Crispin Roderick, CD, was the first Chesapeake to win an AKC all-breed Best in Show, at Lexington Kennel Club in 1975 under judge Len Carey, owner-handled by John Wood. "Cris always thinks he has won even when he hasn't," said owner-handler John Wood. Cris won 35 Group placements, including nine Group I's.

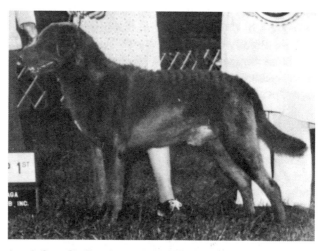

Am. & Can. Ch. Pond View Bolt, CD, WD, owned by William and Ruthann Eller and shown by Ruthann, won the Sporting Group under Kurt Mueller and won Best in Show under Kitty Drury at Kanadasaga Kennel Club.

Ch. Ashby's Chocolate Chip scored an all-breed Best in Show following his National Specialty win at Wilmington Kennel Club in 1976, under Anne Rogers Clark. Owned by John DeVries and handled by Glenn Butler, Chip won a total of 26 Sporting Group placements, including three Group I's.

1976 CH. ASHBY'S CHOCOLATE   John & Christine DeVries
      CHIP
      (Ch. The Queen's Jester ex Ch. Ashby's High Tide)

1978 CH TEAL'S TIGER   Susan Steuben
      (Cinnamon Teal ex Ch. Suzie-Q)

1979 AM. & CAN. CH. CHESRITE'S   Jan Thomas
      JUSTIN TYME, CD, WD
      (Am. & Can. Ch. Donwen's Boo of Tricrown, WD,
        ex Ch. Seamaster's Ginger, CD)

1979 AM. & CAN. CH. EASTERN   Nathaniel Horn
      WATERS' CHARGN
      KNIGHT, CD
      (Ch. Eastern Waters' Oak, CD, TD, WD,
        ex Ch. Eastern Waters' Ever Amber, TD)

1982 CH. SNOCREE'S MAJOR   Dr. Jonathan King
      GUN, WD
      (Snocre's Curly Beau ex Miss Brandee of Four Mile)

1983 CH. DEACON OF THE   Adey Dunnell
      MARSH
      (Von Berg's Mighty Bear ex Sea Tac's Oly Gold)

Am. & Can. Ch. Eastern Waters' Chargn Knight, CD, bred, owned and handled by Nathaniel Horn, the sixth Chesapeake to go Best in Show, at Newcastle (Pa.), 1979, under Peggy Adamson. Chargn had 65 Sporting Group placements, including seven Group I's.

1983   CH. DEACON OF THE MARSH
         (second Best in Show)
1986   AM. & CAN. CH. LIMEFIELD   Marie Whitney Bonadies
         MINE TOO, CD
         (Ch. Fireweed's Wildwood Dusky, CD, WDX,
         ex Am. & Can. Ch. Limefield Magnolia)
1987   CH. CHESTNUT HILLS   Stephanie Carroll
         STONE E'S BRU
         (Ch. Chestnut Hills Stone E's Tug ex Bruiser's Lady Java)

Am. & Can. Ch. Limefield Mine Too, CD, bred and owned by Marie Whitney Bonadies and shown by Jan Thomas, won Best in Show at Valley Forge K.C., 1986, under Mrs. W. P. Wear. "Mintoo" had 58 Group placements including ten Group I awards. He was the first Chesapeake to place in the Group at Westminster K.C.

1988   CH. OAK N THISTLE'S NITTY   James & Brenda Stewart
       GRITTY
       (Am. & Bda. Ch. Ches' True Grit, Am/Bda CD,
         & Am/Bda TD, ex Ch. Crosswinds Flying Cassuth)
1989   CH. WYNDHAM'S   Edward J. Atkins
       CONQUISTADOR
       (Ch. Mister Cahoot Yahoo Von Zybura
         ex Ch. Windown Aelwif of Wyndham)

Ch. Chestnut Hills Stone E's Bru, owned by Stephanie Carroll and handled by Don Cornelius, won Best in Show at Rio Hondo K.C., 1987, under J. White. Bru had 40 Group placements, and was Best of Breed at the 1989 National Specialty Show.

1990	CH FITZHUGH'S BAG THE LIMIT, CD, WDX (Ch. Jacob Duke of Fitzhugh, CD, WD, ex Eastern Waters' Fitzhugh Cuan)	Meghan & Madelyn Conner	
1990	CH. FITZHUGH'S BAG THE LIMIT, CD, WDX (second Best in Show)		
1990	CH. KEPPLE'S BRING IT BACK ZACK (Ch. Wyndham's Algonquin, TDX, WD, ex Kepple's Up and Autumn)	Katherine Kepple-Bowman	
1991	CH. FITZHUGH'S BAG THE LIMIT, CD, WDX (third Best in Show)		

Ch. Oak N Thistle's Nitty Gritty, CGC, bred and owned by veterinarians James and Brenda Stewart, won Best in Show at Annapolis, 1988, under Paul Hipsley, handled by Damara Bolte. Nitty modeled for the statue of the University of Maryland Baltimore County mascot, and took part in its official unveiling.

1992   CH. EASTERN WATERS'   Sarah Horn
         DIAMOND DUST
         (Ch. Riverbend's Norga Wild Rice II
           ex Ch. Eastern Waters' Royal Topaz)

CHESAPEAKE BITCHES WINNING
SPORTING GROUP FIRSTS

1959   Ch. Sampan Sue   Mathias H. Mesdag
1961   Ch. Eastern Waters' Tallapoosa,   Janet Horn
       CD
1989   Ch. Chesapeake Gems Ms Opal   Joanne Permowicz
1990   Ch. Eastern Waters' Keep the   Janet Horn
       Dream

1990	Ch. Eastern Waters' Keep the Dream (second Group First)	
1993	Ch. Sandbar's Coastal Hurricane (Eastern Waters' Scuff Tugboat ex Ch. Eastern Waters' Golden Sands)	Patricia M. Watkins
1993	Ch. Coco's Chocolate Sensation, JH (Ch. Chestnut Hills Stone E's Tug ex Ch. Chelsea's Bold Runner)	Sandra Dietrich & Stephen L. Dietrich
1993	Wyeth Meadows Touch of Amber (Ch. Shorvue's Mr. Bond ex Ch. Fitzhugh's Trinity)	Susan M. Robbins & Donna Lee Molitor

Ch. Wyndham's Conquistador, bred, owned and shown by Edward J. Atkins, won Best in Show at Badger Kennel Club, 1989, in Wisconsin, under Robert Nutbeem.

1993 Ch. Wyeth Meadows Touch Of
Amber
(second Group First)
1993 Ch. Cur-San's Opel of My Eye   Karrie Stevenson
(Cur-San's Copy Tim ex Cur-
San's Suegartree Gemstone)

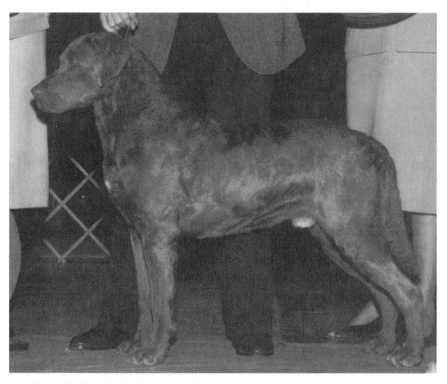

Ch. Fitzhugh's Bag The Limit, CD, WDX, made a record for the breed, winning three Bests in Show. The first, under Anne Rogers Clark, was at Skyline Kennel Club, and the second at James River K.C. in 1990 in Virginia, handled in both shows by John McCartney. "Chase" was bred by Meghan Conner, and is owned by her and Madelyn Conner. At Kennesaw K.C., 1991 in Georgia, he won his third Best in Show, under John D. Rementer, owner-handled by Meghan. With 50 Group placements, including 13 Group I's, Chase came out of retirement to win Best of Breed in the 1992 National Specialty Show.

Ch. Kepple's Bring It Back Zack, bred by Katherine Kepple-Bowman, and owned by her and Karen Friederichsen, won Best in Show at Cambridge, Minnesota, 1990, under Farnandeze Cartwright, Karen Friederichsen handling.

Ch. Eastern Waters' Diamond Dust won Best in Show at Trumbull County, 1992, under Janice Knight. "Dusty" won 12 Group Firsts and is owned by Sarah Horn, and breeder-handled by Nat Horn. He was Best of Breed in the 1988 National Specialty Show.

Dyane Baldwin has been breeding and showing Chesapeakes since 1978. She has trained and handled to titles in conformation, Obedience and Hunting Tests. She is shown here with Ch. Pond Hollow Ketch, a Sweepstakes winner and Sporting Group placer.

16

Grooming and Coat Care

by Dyane Baldwin

THE CHESAPEAKE is one of if not *the* most natural of all Sporting dogs. This not only applies to working abilities but to appearance as well. No frills, feathers or trimming for the Chesapeake! This is a no-nonsense dog with a coat developed for the maximum of purpose and the minimum of care.

Invariably, a puppy buyer new to the breed will ask about grooming instructions. The Chesapeake needs very little. On a weekly basis, nails should be checked and clipped, if needed. Some length helps the dog working slippery banks or going over logs or onto ice in the water. The nail should not be so long as to touch the floor, though. Ears should also be checked and cleaned.

The coat, unless very dirty or in the shedding stage, need not be fussed over. If one brushes, a hound glove with short natural bristles can be used. Wire slicker brushes or shedding and stripping blades should never be used routinely. I have had lovely-coated puppies brought back to me to see, whose coats were brushed daily with a metal brush. All undercoat was gone, and the waving tendency had been brushed out, leaving a Mohawk frizz down the back! I have even seen this damage done using a bristle-type brush too often and too enthusiastically.

A proper time to use metal blades and brushes may be when the coat is shedding. It is then that you will want to get old, dead coat out to encourage the growth of the new one. The coat also takes on a "moth-eaten" look at this time, and brushing will help to even it out. A warm-water bath (no soap), then air drying before you start brushing, will loosen the dead hair and make its removal easier. Once the profuse shedding phase stops, put the metal grooming implements away and wait for the new coat. Depending on coat type and on the individual dog, this usually takes four to six weeks.

What about bathing? Frequent bathing with shampoo is not recommended. A dull coat devoid of natural oils is the result of too many baths. Swimming in *clean* water or hosing/sponging with plain water is usually sufficient. For those times when your dog has found something disagreeable (but obviously delightful) to roll in, use the mildest shampoo you can find. Lanolin shampoos and other types of coat-conditioning shampoos will often make the coat too soft and silky.

SHOW GROOMING

For the show ring, very little additional grooming is needed. A pre-show bath should not be a standard part of your ordinary routine. A quick onceover with a hound mitt before ring-call is usually sufficient. Most people are showing their dogs with whiskers intact, but they can be trimmed if you prefer.

To help a coat look fuller, the day or two before a show, swim, hose or sponge the dog in or with clean water. Let the dog shake out as much as possible. Then take a clean towel and *gently* fluff the coat and allow it to air dry. Once dry, and using your hound mitt again, *gently* brush the coat hairs back in their natural direction. This will create the appearance of more body or fullness.

What about any of the multitude of grooming products sold for the show ring? The Standard describes a harsh outer coat with a thick oily undercoat. Products that promise a bright, shiny coat seem to me to be at odds with this description. A good coat in full bloom has a healthy sheen to it, but no more. Shiny, soft, glistening, etc., are adjectives that do not apply in describing the Chesapeake's coat. So why use products that will create an incorrect appearance?

To the earlier-mentioned puppy owner, I point out that besides the benefits of cost and time, one of the nicest results of this "wash and wear" breed is that you have more time to throw balls, bumpers and birds, which is much more to the Chesapeake's delight than baths and brushing!

CAUTIONS ON COAT CARE

The above article by Dyane Baldwin is directed primarily to the new puppy owner and the novice exhibitor, who need to understand that their Chesapeake is not only different from other breeds, the coat type is unique. Serious, permanent damage to a Chesapeake's coat can result from harsh and excessive use of indiscriminately selected grooming tools, and this is especially hazardous in the puppy, the development of whose adult coat may be irremediably arrested. The Chesapeake does not attain a true coat until the age of two years. Failure to understand the Chesapeake coat comes from ignorance of the work for which the dog is bred, and sometimes leads to serious mistakes by people who are experienced in the care and grooming of other breeds.

Among Sporting dogs, the Chesapeake is one whose condition should permit hunting one day and showing the next, or even on the same day. In the widespread belief that "whiskers are useful and valuable to the dog in work afield, we discourage their removal for show. The Chesapeake needs no embellishment of the natural beauty which results from soundness and elegance of structure, firm muscle tone, the bloom of a healthy coat, the bright and happy disposition and the look of intelligence and alertness that are the indicators of his essential breed character."

Ch. Mitsu Kuma's Saxon Pond, UD, WD. Bred by Sam and Barbara Mullen. Owned by Bill and Dyane Baldwin. Saxon won First places in Novice, Open, and Utility, and a Sporting Group II.

17

Obedience Training

by Betsy Horn Humer

EVERY CHESAPEAKE needs a level of Obedience training regardless of the dog's purpose: show, Field Trial, hunting or pet and companion. The accuracy and depth of understanding depends upon how much you demand. Chesapeakes are smart, and it won't be denied by their owners that sometimes dogs try to run events and think that perhaps some matters would be better done their way. At this point, you must make it clear that the dog is not in charge, but that the owner is.

Basic Obedience training is necessary for all Chesapeakes, regardless of their ultimate function. The American Kennel Club offers different levels of competition. A dog must qualify three times at the Novice (CD) level before advancing to the Open (CDX) level. After Open, the dog may advance to Utility (UD). After the UD, you may choose to continue showing in Open B and Utility B in order to earn points towards an OTCH (Obedience Trial Championship). However, all the exercises taught for the Companion Dog title are useful in everyday life and enable the dog to be a better companion.

Z's Becky, UD, in a portrait by Olan Mills shortly before Becky's death at age nine. Becky was owned by Art and Mary Ellen Mazzola and shown by Mary Ellen.

NOVICE

COMPANION DOG—NOVICE EXERCISES

	POINTS
HEEL ON LEASH & FIGURE EIGHT	40
STAND FOR EXAMINATION	30
HEEL OFF LEASH	40
RECALL	30
SIT-STAY (1 MINUTE)	30
DOWN-STAY (3 MINUTES)	30
TOTAL	200

Heeling, walking or gaiting with the owner is applicable on the street, going into the veterinarian's office, in the field or in the breed ring. The **Stand-Stay** is useful while grooming your dog, during the examination at the veterinarian's and also in the show ring. The **Recall**, or coming when called on the first command, is an essential part of every

Am. & Can. Ch. Sprucegrove's Ruff 'N' Rowdy, UD, SH, WDQ, owned, trained and handled by Mary Nelson. Rowdy was the first Champion of Record to earn a hunting title through the AKC Hunting Test Program. He retired with a Sporting Group First, and one qualifying score toward the Master Hunter title.

dog's daily life. Coming immediately can be a matter of life or death, whether it protects the dog from oncoming traffic or from stray dogs.

Every Chesapeake should be able to sit on command and do a **Sit-Stay**. Your dog should be able to do a Sit-Stay while waiting for you to open the door to go outdoors, and should be able to sit while waiting for dinner or to have a collar and leash put on. Dogs should Sit-Stay with you while waiting to cross a busy street. A Chesapeake has to Sit-Stay in the blind or while working in the field waiting to be sent for a bird. The **Down-Stay** is appropriate behavior while the family eats dinner or sits in the family room.

Ch. Eriez Marsh Hawk, UDT, WD. Bred by Gail Putnam. Owned, trained and handled by Dale Hauer. Marsh earned his CD with a Dog World Award (for scores of 195 or over) in Novice.

Am. Can. & St. Ch. Nuka Bay Toklat, WD, St CD, Am/Can CDX, doing Fly-ball. Note the Agility course in the background. "Tok" was bred, owned, trained and handled by Lynda Barber.

OPEN

The CDX title is a natural for retrievers. Here they are given an opportunity to shine.

COMPANION DOG EXCELLENT—OPEN EXERCISES

	POINTS
HEEL FREE & FIGURE EIGHT	40
DROP ON RECALL	30
RETRIEVE ON THE FLAT	20
RETRIEVE OVER THE HIGH JUMP	30
BROAD JUMP	20
LONG SIT (OUT OF SIGHT—3 MINUTES)	30
LONG DOWN (OUT OF SIGHT—5 MINUTES)	30
TOTAL	200

In the Open class all heeling is *off leash*, which corresponds to field work. The Recall becomes a **Drop on Recall**. In the past this had been a difficult exercise to teach and continue to have the dog perform correctly.

Obedience Training: "Chowder" practicing the Long Down with distractions.

AKC/SKC Ch. Chesagrove's Pinebrook Carrie, CD, CDX, JH, WDX, owned, trained and handled by Shirl Fischer, finished CDX with First Place in Open.

For best results, first teach a random Drop (the dog will "drop" on command in any location) and reward the dog with a ball or food.

The **Retrieve on the Flat** is a natural activity for the Chesapeake. Do retrieves with a wooden or plastic dumbbell. From this retrieve, you progress to the **Retrieve over the High Jump**. The hurdle is set at 1¼ times the dog's height at the shoulders. The dog leaps over the jump to retrieve the dumbbell and then returns over it with the dumbbell. The **Broad Jump** is a long flat jump made up of several boards, which is twice the height of the High Jump. The dog springs in one direction and goes to the handler who is standing at the side of the jump. Most breeds enjoy jumping and as you proceed through the Open routine, the Chesapeake usually gets happier and happier. The **Long Sit-Stay** and **Down-Stays** are longer than in Novice, and the handlers leave the ring and are out of the dog's sight. Stays can present a temporary training problem because your Chesapeake is so bonded to you, but the dog can learn to trust and know that you will return.

Open can become an automatic routine: The dog is told to do one exercise after another and some dogs appear so well trained that they can do the work without a handler or commands.

UTILITY

In contrast, Utility requires decision making on the dog's part. Here is the opportunity to show off the abilities that our breed has. During the following exercises the Chesapeake has to make a choice.

Ch. Chesavieda's Ornamental Buoy, UDT, WDX, the first male Chesapeake to become a Champion UDT. "Ornament" was bred, owned, trained and handled by Dianna Blakey.

Ch. Chestnut Hills Coke, UD, bred, owned, trained and handled by Karen Anderson, won a First place in a combined Utility class under Ben Dale.

UTILITY DOG—UTILITY EXERCISES

	POINTS
SIGNAL EXERCISE	40
SCENT DISCRIMINATION #1	30
SCENT DISCRIMINATION #2	30
DIRECTED RETRIEVE	20
MOVING STAND AND EXAMINATION	30
DIRECTED JUMPING	40
TOTAL	200

Ch. Eastern Waters' Betsy Ross, UD, was Susan Cone's first Chesapeake UD. Sue trained and handled her to all titles.

Heeling becomes a complex **Signal Exercise** in which no voice commands are given. Signals are used to instruct the dog in the positions Heel, Stand, Stay, Down, Sit, Come and Return to Heel, all off leash. **Scent Discrimination**—what a perfect opportunity to demonstrate the excellent nose that our breed has! The dog will work from a group of ten matching articles, half of which are leather and half metal. The dog must select the handler-scented article, leather and then metal, or vice versa. The **Directed Retrieve** is a form of beginning field work at its easiest. The dog must select one of three gloves as directed by the handler. The **Moving Stand** demonstrates that the dog possesses good temperament and trainability by allowing a stranger to approach and examine.

Directed Jumping involves multiple commands. There are two jumps, each on opposite sides of the ring, approximately twenty feet apart. The jumps are 1¼ times the shoulder height of the dog. One is the

191

Ch. Sandy's Hi-Ho Shooting Star, UD, JH, WDX, CGC, bred, owned, trained and handled by Kathy Miller. Star had a great record as an Obedience dog and working gun dog.

familiar **High Jump (Solid Jump)** from the Open class and the other is a **Bar Jump**, which is a bar resting on two uprights. The dog is sent directly away to a distance of approximately forty feet, turns and is told Sit, and is then signaled by the handler as to which jump to take. After jumping, the dog returns directly to the handler. The routine is repeated and the dog is directed to go over the opposite hurdle. Unlike the earlier exercises in Obedience where the dog always has something to retrieve when sent away from you, there is nothing to retrieve. The dog must go to an ''unmarked'' area. As a result, many trainers teach this exercise using food or toys during training, so that the dog has something to go toward in practice.

Throughout Utility the dog has the opportunity to make choices (right or wrong) in most of the exercises. Multiple signals, ten articles, three gloves and two jumps provide many choices and opportunities for error.

To date, Chesapeake Bay Retrievers have maintained a low profile in Obedience competition. AKC records from 1980 to present show the number of dogs earning titles dramatically oscillates from year to year.

OBEDIENCE TRIAL CHAMPION

At present we have one Chesapeake Bay Retriever with an Obedience Trial Championship (OTCH). Few Chesapeakes go on to earn advanced titles. No more than 20 percent of the dogs that earn CDs go on to earn a CDX. Twenty-five percent of the dogs earning CDX titles go on to earn UDs. With only three or four Chesapeakes earning a Utility Dog title every year, there is a very small group of dogs eligible to compete for an OTCH. If you would like to pursue these titles, it is best to look into classes geared at competition training.

WHERE TO TRAIN

Obedience classes can be located by contacting your local dog club, inquiring of your veterinarian or reading the Yellow Pages and the classified section under "Dogs" or "Pets for Sale" in your local newspaper.

Classes are offered by Obedience clubs, kennels and private trainers. They are also offered as adult education courses given through schools, Ys and county park systems. Quality and training methods vary. If you can ask to visit and observe a class beforehand, you will be able to see firsthand the instructor at work and the resulting attitudes of the dogs and trainers. You can learn to train your dog from books, but classes provide a social outlet for you and your dog. The instructor will be able to help you and offer other methods of training, reinforcement and praise, if needed.

Obedience training is changing. In addition to the original school of compulsive training, a school of inducive training has also developed. Chesapeakes, who are devoted and intelligent, may also be sensitive, perhaps not always physically, but mentally. The "stubborn" Chesapeake may be physically tolerant, but not mentally tolerant of compulsive training. Training with positive reinforcements such as food and toys in addition to verbal and physical praise produces a happier worker. Showing the dog what to do instead of forcing it into performing is producing a dog who learns more quickly.

As dogs learn the Obedience exercises, they demonstrate that they know what is expected of them by anticipating commands. Anticipation is part of the learning process. The dog knows in advance what you want and is happy understanding what you want. That dog will demonstrate this understanding by acting independently and doing the exercise before any commands are given.

Even though training has changed, the degrees to be earned are basically the same. If you decide that AKC competition is for you, write to the American Kennel Club, 51 Madison Avenue, New York, N.Y. 10010 and request a copy of the Obedience regulations.

"ABBY," OTCH

BY SUSAN CONE

Ch. Am. & Can. OTCH Katmai Abigail Adams, WD, was bred by Anne Bowen, and was sired by Ch. Rockrun's Kahlua Kobi, CD, out of Ch. Rockrun's Amber Mischief, UD. She is the first Chesapeake to earn the Obedience Trial Championship.

Retired from competition in February 1992 because of a ruptured cruciate ligament, Abby had earned nine Highest Score in Trial awards, eight of them from the advanced classes and nine High Combined awards. She won the ACC Jodri-Nugget-Blaze and Eloise Heller Cherry trophies each three times, as well as the Chesareid Amber Hue and Eastern Waters' Betsy Ross trophies. Competing in three Gaines tournaments, she placed in one.

In quest of the OTCH from earliest puppyhood, Abby has had an outstanding career, earning every title in three straight shows. She won her first High Combined award while legging in Utility A, winning a runoff against Tempe, her half-sister. They are the only two Chesapeakes ever to have earned High Combined awards. She failed only two Stays in six years of extensive showing, in the same place in the Open B ring at South Jersey Kennel Club, where twice she sat up on the Down, scratched and neatly lay down again.

In the torridly hot June of 1991, when she completed her OTCH, her Open B average was 197.36 and her Utility B average 195.8 over eight shows with two High in Trials and three High Combineds. When her career ended prematurely, she had 124 OTCH points.

Ch. Am. & Can. OTCH Katmai Abigail Adams, WD. Bred by Anne Bowen, and owned by Susan Cone and co-owned by Anne. Trained and handled to Obedience and working titles by Sue Cone. Janice Bykowsky helped point "Abby" for her conformation championship. Abby is the first, and, to date, the only Chesapeake to have achieved the Obedience Trial Championship.

Earning the OTCH was a matter of motivation, attention to details and some luck. Abby's structural soundness, coupled with her retrieve drive and natural attentiveness, made it all possible. Her enjoyment of training enabled us to work on the details that go into a winning performance without her becoming stale or bored. The difference between a 195 score and scores of 197 and higher is made up of details: half-point errors accumulate quickly, from split-second lapses of concentration and from small imperfections that can occur.

From the beginning it was important to build Abby's confidence through inducive and positive training. She never feared that making a mistake would lead to a correction, and thus had the security to keep trying to get the work right and earn her reinforcements.

Despite the physical demands of daily schooling, travel and showing, I found competitive Obedience to be largely a mental sport. In training I am continually running mental decision trees: which action to reinforce, and what reinforcers to use. I had to realize when one method of teaching a behavior wasn't working, and try to be creative and flexible enough to try a different approach. I learned very early not to pressure or push Abby, as she would immediately become insecure and work reluctantly.

There is a mental aspect to showing as well. The handler's attitude has a direct bearing on the dog's performance, and confidence and a positive focus are imperative. Relaxation techniques, mental imaging, visualization and positive self-talk have helped me to do justice to a great dog.

I was also lucky to have a great coach, Patty Ruzzo, whose eye for detail added a full point to my heeling score, and many other friends whose advice, support and encouragement helped us reach our goal.

But most of all, it had to be fun for both Abby and me, and it was. The fun came from the communication we achieved and the breakthroughs in training when Abby suddenly understood what I was trying to tell her and began tentatively to make a correct response. The fun came from watching her joyously execute a command, performing an exercise she loved to do with the utmost in willingness and enjoyment and knowing that the exercise had become rewarding in itself.

Though retired, she gets some play training every day, and goes along to shows to visit her friends outside the ring. I'm lucky that Abby and I could travel so far together.

OBEDIENCE HISTORY AND RECORDS
BY BETSY HORN HUMER

Back in 1937, Allein Owens, Jr.'s Bay Bum became the first Chesapeake to receive an Obedience title when he passed the Companion Dog requirements. In 1938, Mrs. Owens and her Daybreak accomplished the same feat. It was 1941 before four more earned their CD titles.

Then the war came along and Obedience, like most dog activities, gave way to the war effort. Only a few dogs competed. But once the country returned to normal, Chesapeake Obedience fanciers resumed their activity. Many owners felt that besides being fun, Obedience work is also a necessary part of properly bringing up a young dog.

To date, through the year-end of 1992, 1,260 Chesapeakes have won their CD title. From the beginning of 1980 until year-end 1992, a total of 736 CDs were earned.

1980—32	1984—64	1988—65	1992—65
1981—43	1985—70	1989—48	
1982—42	1986—59	1990—72	
1983—57	1987—72	1991—47	

The first two Chesapeakes to win the more advanced title of **Companion Dog Excellent**, both in 1943, were: Chessie, owned by Julia Griffith, and Ch. Water Witch, owned by Mrs. Allein Owens, Jr. Only a few dogs each subsequent year passed these difficult requirements. By the end of 1992, the total of Chesapeakes who have earned the CDX stood at 259. From 1980 to 1992, the total of 141 titles were earned. Some kennel names appear multiple times in the listings. Eastern Waters appears the most often with eleven CDX titles. Chestnut Hills dogs had five titles, followed by Chesrite, Meadowood and Rockrun with four titles each. Eriez and Longcove dogs earned a total of three titles.

Seven owners of Chesapeakes each earned three CDX degrees on three different dogs. They are Karen Anderson (Chestnut Hills), Lynda Barber (Nuka Bay), Susan Cone, Brian Cox/Angela Felker (Chesacola),

Ch. Thundrin Jason of Ambersbrew, UDT, JH, WDX, owned, trained and handled by Janet Birk.

Montauk Waters' Tempe Wick, UD, Can CDX, WD, owned by Susan Cone and her daughter, Jennifer, and trained and handled by Susan.

Betsy Humer (Eastern Waters), Jeannie Kinney (Longcove) and Janet LeBarnes.

Utility Dog titles are much harder to obtain, and through the end of 1992, only fifty-three Chesapeakes had passed these rigorous tests. From 1980 to 1992, Susan Cone trained and handled four Chesapeakes to UD titles. Janet LeBarnes earned two UDs on her dogs. Anne Bowen's Ch. Rockrun's Amber Mischief, UD, WD, produced three littermates who earned their UDs: Montauk Waters' Tempe Wick, UD, WD, Ch. Thundrin Jason of Ambersbrew, UDT, JH, WDX, and Ch. Amber's Elsie,

UD, JH, WDX. A second litter out of "Amber" produced "Abby" (Ch. OTCH Katmai Abigail Adams, WD) who went on to earn a fourth UD for Amber's offspring, and eventually became the first Chesapeake Bay Retriever OTCH.

Three Eastern Waters' dogs also earned their UDs. Two were produced by Ch. Eastern Waters' Cadence, CD, owned by Betsy Humer: Ch. Eastern Waters' Sanderling OP, UD, and Ch. Eastern Waters' Tide-runner, UDT, JH, WD.

Of the thirty-six Chesapeakes earning UD titles from 1980 to 1992, twenty-three are also breed champions. In addition, twenty have Working Dog titles (WD or WDX issued by the American Chesapeake Club). Our UD Chesapeakes are truly a talented group of all-around dogs.

UTILITY DOG TITLEHOLDERS

Ch. Eastern Waters' Betsy Ross	05/17/80	(b)	Susan Cone
(Ch.) Jessica Lamb, WDX	02/01/81	(b)	Tobi Carnine
Mount Joy's Sara C	09/26/81	(b)	Roberta Sundrud
Moutauk Waters' Genie	11/07/81	(b)	Jennifer Cone
Ch. Mitsu Kuma's Saxon Pond, WD	05/01/82	(m)	Dyane & William Baldwin
(Ch.) Rockruns Amber Mischief, WD	11/26/82	(b)	Anne Bowen & Paul Allen
Ch. Chestnut Hill's Coke	04/20/83	(b)	Karen Anderson
Poolside's Mark O' the Castle, TD, WD	05/15/83	(m)	L. Vestervelt & Susan La Mielle
Cogley's P R Betsy Ross	09/24/83	(b)	Bill Coryell
Wendy's Miss Autumn Breeze	10/08/83	(b)	Herbert Swinney
Ch. Chesrite's Spec'l Tyme O' Kokos'ng, WDX	10/06/84	(b)	Janet Le Barnes
Just Daisy Mae, TD	04/13/85	(b)	Juliet & Rafael Veve
Ch. Sandy's Hi-Ho Shooting Star, JH, WDX	06/08/86	(b)	Kathy Miller
Ch. Sprucegrove's Ruff N Rowdy, SH, WDX	08/08/86	(m)	Mary Nelson
Montauk Waters' Tempe Wick, (WD)	10/04/86	(b)	Susan & Jennifer Cone
Ch. Longcove's Pine Baron, WD	10/25/86	(m)	Alfred & Jeannie Kinney

Ch. Meadowood's Fair Megan, UD, WD, bred, owned, trained and handled by Sylvia Holderman.

Ch. Thundrin Jason of Ambersbrew, TD, JH, WDX	06/06/87	(m)	Janet Birk
(Ch. & OTCH) Katmai Abigail Adams, WD	05/10/88	(b)	Susan Cone & Anne Bowen
Ch. Noreen's Spice N' Courage, WD	10/30/88	(b)	Noreen Silva
Caroway's Karawa Bay, WD	11/05/88	(b)	Ronald Stoeck
Ch. Hy-Hopes Spec'l Keep'M Guess'n, JH, WD	11/18/88	(m)	Janet LeBarnes
Ch. Amber's Elsie, JH, WDX	11/20/88	(b)	Jan Estes
Ch. Eriez Marsh Hawk, TD, WD	04/25/89	(m)	Dale Righter

Ch. Eastern Waters' Sanderling OP, UD. Bred by Betsy Humer and owned, trained and handled by Lynda Barber.

Ch. Eastern Waters' Sanderling OP	07/30/89	(b)	Lynda Barber
Ch. Meadowoods Fair Megan, WD	10/08/89	(b)	Sylvia Holderman
Ch. Eriez Lady of the Lake	09/09/90	(b)	Gail & Janet Putnam
Crackshot's Firestorm, TD, JH	09/23/90	(b)	Jon & Jean Gravning
Elijah's Sunshine Sarah, WDX	11/24/90	(b)	Vicki Woods
Ch. Eastern Waters' Tiderunner, JH, WD	04/28/91	(m)	Elizabeth & Rupert Humer
Z's Lucy Puddlejumper	04/28/91	(b)	Gretchen Grevelding
Ch. Nesnah's Shadow B's Mr. Walnut, TDX, JH, WD	06/09/91	(m)	Stephanie Adelmann
Blustrywoods Double Shot	11/09/91	(m)	Kathy Perry & David Fahner

U-CD Ch. Eastern Waters' Tiderunner, UDT, JH, WD, Can CDX. "Tide" was bred, owned and trained to all titles by Betsy Humer. He is her husband's favorite hunting dog.

Ch. Ragin Cajun Meagan	02/29/92	(b)	Angela Felker & Brian Cox
Cho Cho San	04/05/92	(b)	Eve Broome
Ch. Chesareid Ginger, CDX, TDX	07/05/92	(b)	Dean & Sally Diess
Ch. Brackenwoods Spartan	11/14/92	(d)	Wayne Morie

Ch. Longcove's Pine Baron, UD, WD, costumed with breeder-owner-trainer-handler Jeannie Kinney to show "Native American" origin of the breed, winning in "Lady and Her Dog" contest at Valley Forge Kennel Club show.

Ch. Bayberry Pond Lady, CDX, JH, TD, WD. Bred by Gail Putnam. Owned by Erik Lundberg and Pat Comly. Trained and handled in conformation and to Hunting Test title by Dyane Baldwin. Trained and handled in Obedience, Tracking and Working tests by Erik.

18

Tracking with Your Chesapeake

by Mildred G. Buchholz

NO ONE trains a dog to track in the sense we generally think of as training—the dog already knows very well how to track. Rather, you must consider that you are teaching your dog to use this skill on command, with control and dedication. The two of you must learn to work together—the foundation for the most important ingredient, *a trust in each other*.

It is absolute fact that any dog can track regardless of conditions and circumstances if fortunate to have a handler who will let the dog work his/her own way.

If you are a person who doesn't use common sense in teaching a dog to work for you, regardless of the type of work—control training, field work, etc.—save yourself some time. Don't read on, as Tracking will defeat you. It will take work on your part to teach the dog to follow a specific trail, to work on command and under control. You will learn to believe in your dog's ability as this happens; then comes *trust*. This trust is a two-way deal; it is equally important that the dog trusts you. This factor cannot be overemphasized. A lack of it will lead to a million excuses and reasonings as to why the dog failed to be successful on track!

Remember your dog *can* track, you don't have to teach Tracking.

But you do have to initiate the idea and dog's desire *to want to track* that trail now, and to "*stay on track.*" This is where you must have the ability to get across what it is you want your dog to do.

Tracking is the most enjoyable and rewarding experience you will ever share with your dog. How impressive it is to watch a trusting handler and dog team. The dog is a picture of drive and purpose; the handler, confidence and assurance. Chesapeakes are extremely natural in Tracking. This is in their breeding, but it is possible to motivate any dog of sound temperament to want to work for you if your approach is "common sense in teaching." Teaching is understanding, which is the only proper approach to the teaching of anything.

Fact number two, and this may be my farewell to some of you. You cannot *force* a dog to track. Those of you who depend on this approach in training your dog, now will realize why I state you are not training your dog to track, you are teaching your dog to track. *No dog has ever been successfully force-trained to track.*

TRACKING EQUIPMENT

You can accomplish the Tracking title, in many cases, almost entirely by yourself with your dog. You don't need assistants or intricate, expensive equipment.

The dog will work in a harness, and in a very short time, associate Tracking with the harness. The harness, usually made of leather, should be comfortable and nonrestricting. You can often find a suitable harness in a pet section of a drug store or department store, or have one custom-made for your dog at a leather or harness shop.

You will need a six-foot lead and a thirty-to-forty-foot lead. Your long lead should be of nylon webbing, heavy enough not to blow easily in the wind and smooth enough to slide through brush and high cover. You will find it wise to select your "long lead" carefully, as it will improve your handling 100 percent. Add to your collection eight to ten stakes or markers. These again you must select with some foresight. You want them to be about three feet high, visible to you and of a material that will slide into the ground easily and be durable for many years of Tracking.

Chesapeakes are naturally quick to spot anything flapping (such as a flag) in the distance and I would advise not using any material at the top of your markers. Some suggestions: three-quarter-inch wooden dowels with one end pointed and the top end painted a bright color, or PVC pipe cut in lengths of three feet is excellent. Garden stakes or archery arrows with metal tips can also be used. Test the ground where you live and see which type of stake seems suitable; you want to be able to walk along and place the marker securely without having to stand there pounding it into the ground. They should be visible to you at about one hundred yards and not too obvious to the dog. When you have selected the best type for your ground conditions, make up a set of eight or ten and have them with you on all training sessions. You will also need a leather glove or similar leather article, and you will soon be adding various different items to your collection. Equipment now assembled and ready, it's time to learn to "lay a track."

THE TRACK

In Tracking, a main factor is to keep the dog directly on the ground scent put down as you walked. You cannot do this unless you know exactly where the track is yourself. I would suggest you take yourself out for a few lessons without the dog. Place a marker in a field, indicating your start, walk ahead in a straight line for about fifty to sixty paces and drop a dime; turn and come back directly to the marker. Drive off and come back in ten minutes, start at your marker and see if you can walk out and find your dime! You will find yourself quickly learning to select landmarks you will remember and to walk a straight line. A field that looks fairly nondescript soon has many landmarks to a trained eye. An excellent tracklayer is basic for training a good dog and handler team. This cannot be overemphasized in your foundation work with the dog. If you plan to work with a friend as a tracklayer, safeguard your friendship by seeing that both of you learn to be good tracklayers.

Scent, as we think of it, is not necessarily the way it is for the dog. However, if you understand and believe a few basic facts, you can eliminate a great many of what appear to *you* to be problems, but which are *not* to the dog.

1. Each and every human has a different "scent," just as we all have different fingerprints. The dog has the ability to instantly discriminate and sort these out.
2. No other strong odor can cover scent to the degree that your dog cannot follow the underlying scent. Eliminating misconceptions, you will find yourself gaining confidence as you realize how truly remarkable this is. If I could keep you feeling this way,

Tracking would be a breeze. The very first time you announce you are about to teach your dog Tracking you will find an expert at your elbow just dying to send you into deep depression with theories of wind velocity, ground temperature versus air temperature at various ratios, etc. Their theories will range from the most scientific to the absolutely ridiculous, and make you feel you have to enroll for a Ph.D. in science before taking the first step in harness. My advice to you is quite simple—tune them out, remain steady "on course," believe, have patience and faith, and you will find your dog has the ability also.

3. In the first stages of training it is not necessary to work with another person; you can do all the foundation work yourself. Remember, a dog can discriminate different human scents, so switching to a stranger is no problem once the dog understands what to do and responds eagerly to your commands.

COMMANDS

Your voice and commands, as in all training, must convey your sincere feelings. The starting command should be a phrase such as "Go find it," or "Hunt for it," in a low, excitable tone. In the actual American Kennel Club Tracking test you are allowed to give verbal encouragement as often as you like. You can also *verbally* correct or reprimand the dog in a quiet manner. You will develop these things during your practice sessions. An example of a verbal reprimand: If the dog becomes intrigued with some foreign matter during the track to the point of interfering with concentration, you would say "NO, LEAVE IT," in a firm tone, and the dog should know exactly what you mean and respond. If a dog is going too fast and hard on the track, you must teach the word "Easy" to slow the pace.

"Find it" or "Track" will always mean keep your concentration, keep your nose down and work close. Encouragement, even in very difficult situations, can often be the deciding factor in a *pass* or *fail*. Learn this well and be very careful not to show a hint of impatience in your voice. Your calm voice saying "That's it. Good"—"Work it out. Good." is what's needed.

There is no time limit in an AKC Tracking test, as long as the dog is working. Remember that *no judge can fail you if your dog is on track and working*. Learn to keep your dog working instead of quitting, and learn to *shut up* and not break concentration with constant chatter.

This communication will come easily between you if you start it from the beginning and are constantly teaching association with the phrase and tone followed by praise. The nicest part of competing for your Tracking degree is the complete naturalness you are allowed to have with your dog, compared to the single commands of the Obedience ring. Do not use the dog's name during Tracking, as it will divert attention back to you. Do not use the word "Come," as again you do not want your dog coming back to you, or concentrating on you.

IN THE FIELD

It's time now to head for the fields. You do not need virgin acreage, but do use guidelines for *starting* the beginner dog: 1) Choose a cool time of day, either early morning or evening, before dark; 2) dampness is in your favor; 3) select a quiet area with short, plush grass, such as a lawn; 4) a very windy day is not the best for a newcomer; 5) always bring fresh water for your dog's comfort.

Your first few lessons will only require an area seventy-five yards by seventy-five yards. A golf course just before dark is ideal, or a school-yard after the kids have gone home, or a large corporation front lawn after closing.

Select something your dog enjoys and will get excited to "Go find." This could be a toy or anything that will make a dog want to go out, hunt and find. Having found your location, and arriving in a confident frame of mind, park the car and get your six-foot lead, two markers and the selected item together. Put your dog in harness, hook the lead to the plain collar and tie the lead securely to something close to where you will start the track and the dog can watch what you are doing. Walk away to your start and put your marker in. Stand there and talk to your dog, show the article, enthusiastically trying to focus interest on you and what you are doing. Carrying the article and the second marker, walk slowly out about thirty paces. Place the second marker and continue five to ten more steps, turn and face the dog. Wave the article and while talking, put the article down and sit on it for a count of ten, walk back to the start, using your markers to keep you *on course*.

Go over to the dog and hook the lead to the harness. Holding the dog by the collar, head up, go to within a foot of the marker and allow the dog to sniff around. You must be patient as you try to create interest in the ground where you stood at the start. You may have to literally go for a walk down the path to the article, feeling like you have accomplished nothing. Your first lesson is simply to get the idea across that there is something out there. When the dog comes to the article, either by tracking like a champ or because the two of you came upon it on your walk through the markers, you must give your dog a great deal of *genuine* praise. Throw it or play tug with it, anything that is exuberant and makes it fun to have found it.

Leave your markers in place and come back to the start with the dog and the article. Again, tie the lead to a stake, stand at the start, talk and walk the same course again. If it went well the first time, go twenty steps beyond your last drop and place the article, sit on it, talk and walk back through the markers. Go again, same as before. If eager to move on down the track and out in front and pulling, the dog will have to be restrained slightly from pulling so hard. Every time your dog's head comes up (to visually try and find it), stand still and verbally caution "Track," refusing to go until the dog's head goes down to the ground scent; praise quietly and begin to move again, saying "Good, that's right."

During your first three days of teaching, lay three to four tracks in this same manner each day. Remember, the article at the end is the pot of gold, the finale of the track, and you must strongly make the dog feel like a super dog to find this thing.

At the end of three days, having followed instructions to a "T," even the most unsure dog should be moving on down the track in front of you. Maybe your dog will not be pulling, and still is easily distracted and looking to you for reassurance, but indicating to you a definite improvement from the first day on the first track. Do not be discouraged, for you have accomplished a great deal and are well on your way. But do not go on to anything but a straight track until this dog *is* moving out front, concentrating and responding to your encouragement to "Track."

Soon after the third day you will be up to one hundred yards on a fresh track. Your progress from here out will be determined solely by the dog's attitude. You must determine this for yourself. You should know your own dog's personality, and enthusiasm or lack of enthusiasm should be obvious to you. *As in all training, do not proceed to the next plateau unless the dog is confident at the phase.* A new dog starting in Tracking will usually weave back and forth across the actual track; this is quite natural and will diminish with more experience. Eventually the dog will be driving hard and true on the actual track. Very often a dog will stop and study something, the significance of which is not obvious to you. Allow this check and study for a few seconds, stay quiet, then say "Leave it" and "Track close."

This is an important part of communication—you *do not* know for

Flying D's Semi Sweet, CDX, owned by Tracy Vischer, "hot on the track." A demonstration of a dog pulling into the harness.

Here, Semi Sweet completes her track, bringing the glove to Tracy.

sure what went on there and on a blind track you *absolutely do not* know; the tracklayer could have dropped something or a mouse in season may have left her calling card there. Do not be quick to take verbal action. Communicate your trust but quietly remind the dog to work. You will soon find your dog appreciating your understanding and continuing to work.

You must realize on a blind track that a dog *could* be hung up working a turn and should not be worried about being pressured to "Get to work." Naturally, if this dog stops on a track and is obviously sniffing animal droppings, or staring off at something going down the road, your tone would firmly say "Leave it alone," and "Get back to work." All these things begin in your first few days of tracking and will continue all through your training.

MOVING ON

Chesapeakes are very quick to enjoy Tracking and soon are trying to take you out for a drag; you must hold them back, slow their pace and teach them the word "Easy." This is for their own good, as they will also outrun their nose by thirty to forty yards before they realize the track stopped going straight and took a turn. Once an eager tracker, a Chesapeake very seldom needs to be reminded to "Track" or "Go find it"—enthusiasm is very often the difficulty. Help from the beginning, don't wait for developing problems; slowing down is all that is needed.

When your dog is doing one hundred yards with great drive and concentration (usually within a few days), it is time to put in a turn. Place your marker at the start, walk out about fifty yards and put another marker; walk five more steps and turn 135 degrees to the right or left, continue another thirty paces and place a third marker. Go another five to ten paces and place the article. Walk your track exactly back to the start. By this time your dog will not be watching you lay the track. Begin as usual, and you will now see if your dog has already begun the habit of just driving in a straight line. If so, the dog will shoot past the turn without so much as a nod. If this happens don't go more than twenty paces from your second marker. Back up so *you* are before the marker and the dog is just ahead of it; say "Track close" firmly. It is very important that your dog discovers this independently *and* makes the commitment of the direction of the turn without your guidance. The dog must actually *take* you on that first turn. Then pour on the praise.

It is quite natural for a dog in the beginning stages to circle a great deal at the point of a turn, checking thoroughly both sides before deciding on the direction. You must be patient—and your dog must believe that you will be patient; these are the things that you are subtly doing to build the trust in each other. If the dog stops or circles, be very conscious that you are remaining in the straight-ahead position. Do not find yourself facing various directions and simply following your dog. If you do this you are subconsciously guiding. The first time you run a blind track you will not know where the turn is and won't dare turn in any direction, and your dog may be relying on that cue, which you have subconsciously given in your practice sessions.

212

From here on you will increase the length of your tracks—the amount of 90-degree turns, and the age of the track. You will also be using the long lead around twelve to fifteen feet and learning to handle the lead without becoming hopelessly entangled. Hold the lead at waist level; this is the most comfortable position for you and gives you strong communication from the dog. You must feel through the lead what your dog is telling you, which is why a Tracking dog must be pulling and keeping the line tight. The minute it goes slack, stop; stay straight, and wait for the pull again, either straight ahead or in the direction of the turn. A well-trained dog will leave no doubt in your mind when telling you where to go next. Increase all your steps sensibly, remembering that you are building a mutual confidence. You will have lost the communication between you if you rush your schedule.

Once your dog is thoroughly eager to track, switch to the leather glove for the article, and insist that your dog indicate it to you in some way. The dog does not have to retrieve the glove but you do want a positive indication. There is absolutely no sense in doing an entire difficult track with ease only to have the dog miss the glove at the end. This would fail your entire performance: Your dog *must* indicate the article.

Ch. Chesachobee's Oviedo Millie B, UDT, WD, one of Diney Blakey's well-trained and -handled Obedience and Tracking contestants.

At various points in your training have someone lay a one-turn blind track. Go back on your own for a while again, then a two-turn blind track. These blind tracks will be the best confidence builder for *you* and it's best to do them in easy stages as you progress in your schedule. Once the dog is tracking with vigor (only work about twice a week), it should always be a highlight of the week for both of you. Once you are doing full five-hundred to six-hundred yard tracks, aged over an hour, once a week is enough. Be sure you test your dog's ability in many different areas, different cover, changes of cover, different terrain, under many weather conditions and at different times of the day or night. Use different tracklayers (make sure they know what they are doing) and have many distractions.

In a test, one or both of the judges will follow right behind you during parts of the track, or during the entire track. Your dog must be at ease with people around. As in all training, have your dog completely reliable and very well prepared for a test situation.

There will be a time when the dog settles into tremendous reliability and your confidence is 100 percent. Then you will go out one day and have your dog *appear* to completely blow it, something you simply cannot justify in your mind. Don't try to, and don't worry about it. There are times when it will simply be something you cannot understand. Can you put nose to the ground and track? Don't worry about that isolated incident or let it lessen your confidence in your dog's ability.

There is no possible way I can tell you how long it will be before you are ready for a test. But you will have walked many, many miles of tracks in practice, and only *you* will know when you have thoroughly prepared yourselves for any situation. Tracking is not an easy title and should be well deserved. Most tests have a maximum of ten to twelve dogs and it is totally unfair to enter one in hopes of lucking through it. I strongly recommend your reading and having in your personal library for constant reference the book *Go Find*, by L. Wilson Davis, published by Howell Book House. Also, send for a copy of the AKC's *Tracking Regulations*, which you can request free from the American Kennel Club, 51 Madison Avenue, New York, N.Y. 10010. Additional books that will be useful are *Tracking Dog*, by Glen Johnson, published by Arner Publications, and *Tracking from the Ground Up*, by Sandy Ganz and Susan Boyd.

Now that you are on the way to becoming an expert, it's time you learned the vocabulary of your newfound sport:

First and Thirty. Means the starting flag and thirty yards in the

DOG'S CATALOG # _____ TRACK # _____ TOTAL YARDS _____

Chart the track in solid line on graph below: chart the dog's course
in broken line (use ballpoint pen and bear down.)

N

Indicate North with an
arrow inside of circle.

Passed or failed _____

Time tracklayer started _____

Dog's starting time _____

Dog's finishing time _____

Ground Conditions _____

Weather Conditions _____

Wind Direction & Speed _____

If dog is absent, mark "absent" on this page.

I hereby certify that I have judged the above dog after having read the instructions on the cover of this
book and followed them out to the best of my ability.

_____
Judge's Signature

direction of the track. First and Thirty is telling you actually where the track is for thirty yards, after that you are on your own.

Cover. Vegetation—some sites have sparse or light cover, while others are dense and plush.

Change of Cover. Means the track goes from a clover field to a thicket-type cover.

Leg. Means the distance between one turn on the track and the next turn.

The Drop. Article left at the end of the track.

Blind Track. A track that the handler and dog have not seen laid and they will run the track with no knowledge of its layout other than the First and Thirty.

Plotting. One or both of the judges must personally lay out each track a day or more before the test with the help of the club members holding the test. This plot then is charted on a map showing yardage of each leg, turns and drop with landmarks for the judges to use in their reference.

Laying Tracks or Tracklayer. On the day of the test, the person called the tracklayer will walk each track, using the map and removing all markers except the First and Thirty, and leave the article (*The Drop*).

Cross Track. Something (animal or person) other than tracklayer that crossed over the laid track.

Flags. Same as a marker; used in giving direction of the plotted track.

Fresh Track. The dog runs the track soon after the tracklayer walks the course.

Aged Track. Time lapse after the track has been laid. Example: aged thirty minutes, aged two hours, etc.

Passed. Both judges must agree that the dog worked out the course of the tracklayer and indicated the article to the handler, who in turn shows it to the judges.

TD Title. That's the one we're after! This title may be earned at any time after six months of age, either before, in the middle of or after any other titles awarded by the American Kennel Club.

Certify or Certification. A statement dated within one year of the Tracking test, which is signed by a licensed American Kennel Club judge who has seen the dog work to satisfaction and feels the dog is ready to enter a test. This statement must accompany your entry to the test.

Tracking Judges. Deemed by the American Kennel Club as qualified to understand various conditions that exist when a dog is working a scent trail such as weather, lay of land, cover and wind. They must have a thorough knowledge of dogs working under various conditions.

Whistle. Left to the end, in hopes that you will never have to know what it is. The judge will blow the whistle if the dog is too far off track or has lost interest, meaning "back to the drawing board" or that you have *failed*.

To round out your expertise, some things about the weather that might help you out while you are Tracking:

1. Dew on the grass at night or in early morning is a sign of fair weather (dew forms only when air is dry, skies are clear).
2. When distant sounds are loud and hollow, look for rain.
3. Birds perch more before a storm because low pressure air is less dense, making it harder to fly.
4. Smells are stronger before rain.
5. High clouds won't rain on you no matter how threatening they look.
6. Rising smoke foretells fair weather.
7. Face the wind and the storm will always be on your right.

Tracking is a great deal of work, time-consuming, great fun (it *must* be) and very rewarding. It would have to be compared to the confidence and trust the blind have in their guide dogs. When taught to track in this manner—in harness, on lead, disciplined and under control, taught to follow the ground scent—a dog cannot possibly confuse his Tracking with any other type of work.

Ch. Nesnah's Shadow B's Mr. Walnut, UDTX, JH, WDX, owned, trained and handled by Stephanie Adelmann. "Wally" is the first Champion, Utility Tracking Dog Excellent (UDTX) Chesapeake.

19

Advanced Tracking and the TDX Title

by Sally Diess

NOW THAT YOUR CHESAPEAKE has successfully completed a Tracking test and earned a TD, does all the fun have to stop? No! One of the biggest challenges of your life could be just ahead for you and your dog.

A TDX track is much more than simply a longer TD track. The total distance does increase from 440 to 500 yards to 800 to 1,000 yards, but many varied and interesting things happen on or to the track on the way to the final drop. The time lapse from when the tracklayer walks the track, to the time the dog is put on the track is one significant difference. For the TD, most tracks are run at thirty- to fifty-minute time lapse, which in most cases is considered a "hot scent." The dog is taking cues directly from the scent the tracklayer leaves as he/she walks along.

For a TDX, the time lapse is usually three to four hours, which requires more concentration on the part of the dog to pick up clues from the environment near the track as well as on the track itself. Air currents caused by contours of the land and wind have an effect on where to find the scent after a few hours. The dog has to rely on other factors that make up the scent, such as crushed vegetation, rather than only the scent of the tracklayer, but must still be able to pull out the tracklayer's scent. This is in order to distinguish it from the scent of the two cross-tracklayers

Ch. Wyndham's Algonquin, TDX, won Best of Breed, and his dam Ch. Windown Aelwif of Wyndham, Best of Opposite Sex, ACC Specialty Show 1980. "Griff" was bred by Edward J. Atkins, and jointly owned by him and Helen Szostak. They both showed him to many Sporting Group awards including 5 Group I's. Helen trained him in tracking, and he was the first Chesapeake to earn a TDX.

who will cross the track in two widely separated places about 1½ hours after the tracklayer has laid it. The dog must not be put off by changes in cover, and must be able to change from light to heavy cover or the opposite without losing the trail or refusing to enter it.

In a TD, ideally, the whole track is laid in one type of cover with no obstacles that would make going or scenting difficult. In a TDX, at least two areas of difficulty must be included on the track. Areas of difficulty can include many things and vary from location to location depending on what the judges have to work with. Some common ones include crawling through fences, crossing shallow streams, negotiating deep gullies, tracking across rock surfaces and roads, climbing over logs or winding through heavy brush—anything that would safely present a scenting or physical challenge to the dog.

If that were not enough, the dog is asked to find two small, personal-type articles on the track besides the final drop, which is usually a glove or wallet. These personal articles can include such things as a sock, glasses case, handkerchief, comb, brush, checkbook cover or belt. A somewhat larger article is left at the starting stake, which the handler can carry on the track to refresh the dog's memory of the scent if necessary. These are sometimes caps or slippers.

Another significant difference in TDX is the way you approach the starting stake and start your dog. In the TD, you have a starting stake and a directional stake thirty yards farther on in the direction of the first leg. The TDX has only the starting stake, and you will be directed how to approach it so that the direction of the first leg could go anywhere within a 180-degree radius from the stake and not in the direction that you are heading when you approach it. Your dog should actually be searching for the direction of the first leg before approaching the flag and should have found it before you pass by it and pick up the starting article.

TDX—STEP BY STEP

Training your Chesapeake for the TDX is best taken one step at a time. Generally you start with either time or distance, and there is no reason why you can't do them interchangeably—just don't try to add both

Cub's Bloody Red Baron, CD, TDX, WDX, and Ch. Chesareid Ginger, UDTX, owned by Dean and Sally Diess. Baron got his TDX in 1985, and Ginger in 1989, both trained by Sally. Sally has had Chesapeakes since 1969, and she entered her first AKC Tracking Test in 1980. Since then she has put TDs on four of her Chesapeakes and TDXs on two so far. She became an AKC Tracking judge in 1987, and TDX judge in 1993.

time and distance in the same track when first starting TDX work. For instance, you have just passed the TD and you and your dog are enjoying it so much that you want to do more, so you start to gradually lay longer and longer tracks that are about the same difficulty as what you have been doing for TD work. Make some of the legs of the track longer and/or put in a few more turns. TDX tracks are required to have five to seven turns. When you have worked up to one thousand yards with the dog still going strong, go back to a five hundred-yard track and gradually start aging the tracks up to two or three hours before adding age to your longer tracks.

At some point during this aging process, usually at forty-five minutes to ninety minutes, you will experience with your dog what is commonly called "going over the hump." This means that your dog changes from the "hot scent" technique of scenting to the "aged scent" technique. The weather and ground conditions will play a part in at what age of track this will take place at. If it is hot and dry it will occur earlier than if it is cool and damp. You will notice that the dog will find it harder to concentrate on "the track," and may look around for something fresher or get distracted easier by little critters and their holes. It usually makes it necessary for a dog to work harder and more thoroughly to pull out the scent. If the wind is blowing, you may notice more back and forth work as the dog checks areas where the scent has been blown to and pooled and then back to the actual track. This is especially apparent when hedges or bushes are in the vicinity of the track.

Older Tracks

Once your dog is comfortable with three-hour-old tracks, going beyond that time by a few hours does not seem to make too much difference to the dog. That is, if not too much else has happened to the track. Just for your own confidence, you should experience a few five-to-eight-hour-old tracks so you know your dog could do it. Depending on your schedule, you may have to practice on longer tracks. I used to lay a track on my lunch break and then run my dog on it when I got off work. This was usually a four-hour age. If someone else did this for me it was usually a five-to-six-hour age. The difference this additional time makes to the dog depends on what kinds of things happened to the track during this time rather than just the aging process, once the dog has learned to work an aged track. For instance, a track laid in an unused field when the weather remains the same will most likely present fewer problems for a dog several hours from the time it was laid than one laid in a public park next to a jogging trail when a storm with high winds came along.

FLAGS

Early on in your beginning TDX work, back when you are starting to increase either time or distance, you should make a session out of getting your dog accustomed to starting off just one flag (the starting post). You will set up four or five starting flags with a starting article and a seventy-five to one hundred-yard leg with a glove at the end in different places or fields so that the dog cannot see more than one of them at a time. For the purpose of this exercise, aging isn't important. You are teaching the dog to find the track from one pole and to find the direction by searching around the pole to see which way the person who left the article at the pole went. This exercise would be best done with a helper to be your tracklayer, but could be done by yourself if necessary.

You will now approach the first flag with your dog from a different direction than the tracklayer to about twenty yards from the flag. From here, not at the flag, you check harness and line to be sure you are ready to start. From here you tell the dog "Track" and let him/her approach the pole. Many dogs, even in their TD work, start tracking before they approach the first flag and do not want to be delayed at the starting flag to gather the scent. For these dogs, the light has already dawned that the tracklayer walks up to the pole and past it when starting a track; he or she doesn't drop out of the sky at the starting flag and go from there. At this point, if your dog seems confused at this premature start twenty yards or so from the flag, walk up to the starting flag, show the article to sniff and encourage the dog to circle the starting flag trying to find the track. Point the track out if need be. Find the article at the end and do whatever you do at the end of a track to keep up the Tracking motivation. Show the dog that it is just a new way of starting.

Now go on to the next start and try again giving the dog a chance to start again independently. Help out only if and when it is needed. Always make a big deal over finding the glove and going on to complete the series of starts. As you work through the series, make a point of approaching the starting flag at different angles to the track (see **Figure 1, next page).** It will probably not be necessary, but if the dog still hasn't caught on by the end of the series, do the series over sometime in the next few days. After this, always start your dog in this manner.

NEW CONCEPTS—ADDING ON

You are now aging your full-length tracks and your dog knows how to find the direction of the track from a single starting flag. Now it is time

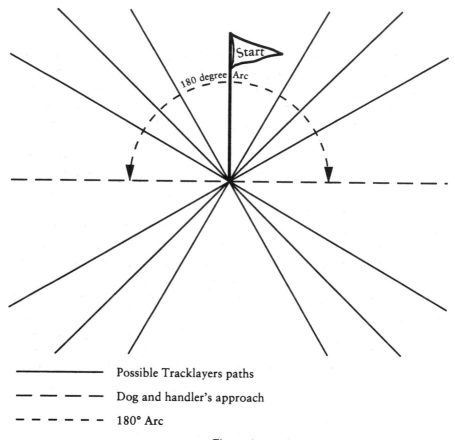

Possible Tracklayers paths

— — — — Dog and handler's approach

- - - - - 180° Arc

Figure 1

to start adding new things to the track one at a time by the "saturation" or "overkill" method. I like to use this method when introducing multiple articles on the track and cross-tracks especially. It is also useful in getting the idea across to the dog that tracks can be followed across roads, creeks, plowed or bare ground, or at least picked up on the other side.

Multiple Articles

You can add new things in any order. Just so you work on only one new concept at a time. Let's start with multiple articles. In the TD, there was only one article and it was at the end of the track. When the dog found it, that was all. Then you introduced another article at the beginning of the track and that article indicated what scent to look for in order to find the article at the end.

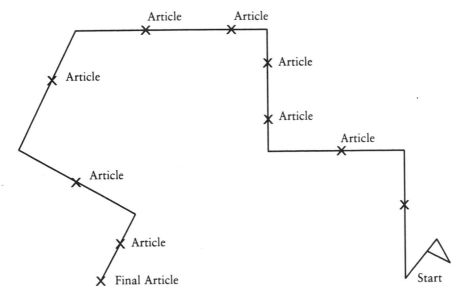

Figure 2

In a regulation TDX track, there will be two more articles on the track and we neither want the dog to ignore these articles nor quit after finding the first or second one. I believe the quickest way to get this idea across to the dog is to put up to ten articles on the track—perhaps one or two on every leg. Repeat this procedure as many times as is necessary to get the dog to indicate the article and then go on tracking to find another article **(see Figure 2).**

Your Chessie will probably either fetch the article and come running back to you ready for a game or a treat because he/she has found "the article" or ignore the article, which probably isn't nearly as interesting as the usual glove and not give you any indication whatsoever. In the first case, you stop on the track and take the article from the dog, praising profusely and giving a small tidbit, but save the retrieving or tugging games to the end.

Then encourage the dog to start tracking again. If you stay put on the track, it shouldn't take the dog long to find the track and get going again. If the dog has trouble getting started, try to use the starting article again, and say "Track." If this doesn't work, point to the track and walk a few paces until your Chessie picks up the track. In the second case where the dog ignores the article and just keeps on tracking, stop as soon as you see the dog has gone past it and encourage by saying "Find it." If that doesn't work, walk up to the article, point to it and say "Fetch" or whatever you have your dog do to indicate an article. You may have

225

to go back to food in or under the article to at least get the dog to check it out. Continue on throughout the track in this manner until the dog gets the idea to *indicate all* the articles on the track, no matter how uninteresting. The dog must continue tracking until the last article you are looking for is indicated. Remember, dogs can "indicate" in a number of ways. Some only give it a poke; some will pick it up and carry it a few feet and then drop it. It is wise to teach the dog to indicate the article in some obvious way. You don't want to leave any doubt in the judges' minds whether the dog saw the article or if you just picked it up as you ran over it.

Cross-Tracks

When you are comfortable with the way your dog indicates articles and gets started again, you are ready to introduce something else. Let's take cross-tracks next. As with the articles, you are going to set up a practice situation where the dog will encounter cross-tracks numerous times on one track so that you can see how the dog handles a cross-track and you can help get past it in a controlled setting. You will need the help of at least one other person and two or three if you can get them for this exercise. You will need to set up a track as shown in **Figure 3**. It is a good idea to mark your corners and where the cross-track crosses the main track in some way so you know exactly where it is. If you have enough people to help, have another person lay the main track and two other people, walking at arm's length apart, make the cross-track.

The main track is laid first and the cross-track is laid an hour to an hour and a half later. You will start your dog when the track has aged at least two hours and preferably three hours. Watch to see what happens as your dog comes to the first cross-track. Does the dog a)—ignore it, b)—think it is a corner and go for it or c)—check it out for a few feet either or both ways and then disregard it for the original track? Hopefully your Chessie will either ignore it or just check it out for a short distance. If either occurs, quietly confirm that the right choice was made and carry on to the next crossing.

If this is treated as a corner and your dog then gets more than ten to fifteen yards off the main track, go back and show the main track ahead and that you want this dog to follow only that one. Then see what happens at the next crossing. Continue on until the drop at the end and reward your dog in your usual manner. Usually one time through this pattern is all it takes to get the point across, but don't hesitate to set it up again if somewhere down the line your dog has problems with cross-tracks. If you work alone a lot and don't have the opportunity to have your tracks

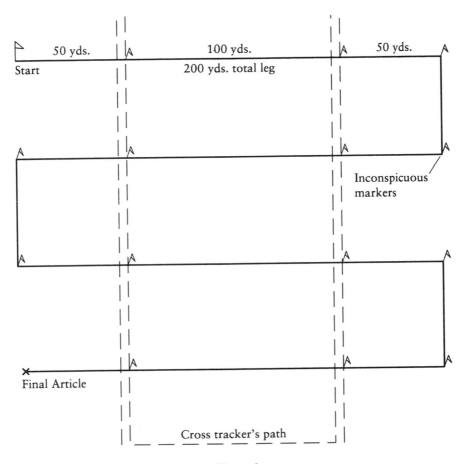

Figure 3

cross-tracked regularly, try to get someone to do a simple cross-track for you once in a while or lay your track across a known path where someone could incidentally cross it.

You can use the same idea to get your dog used to the idea to cross roads, areas of bare or plowed ground or streams. If the dog loses the scent, crossing a stream for instance, teach him/her to look for it on the other side, and carry on.

Changing Cover

Now you are ready to make your tracks more challenging with changes of cover and a great variety of areas of difficulty. You will find yourself always on the lookout for new places to try, especially if it presents a new challenge. The more variety of terrain, cover and obstacles that you can train on, the more confident both you and your dog will feel at a test. Don't forget to train in a variety of weather conditions also.

To be more specific, your dog should not hesitate to plunge into chest-high tules near a pond from a cut hay field or into leaf-covered woods from a wild meadow or sand and sage brush from an alfalfa field or across plowed or bare ground or wood chips. A passable fence, a stream of water, plowed or bare ground, or a log that has to be scrambled over should not discourage a dog. A road or deep gully or footbridge should not be a problem, nor should going through passable brush. If any of these things are a problem to your dog when first encountered work it through, encourage and show your dog how to work it out. Also show that you expect the dog to search for the track.

If you know you are likely to encounter certain types of terrain, cover or obstacles at certain tests, try to work your dog on something similar so you are both confident when you come across that particular element in a test. This includes weather conditions. Wind and wind patterns on certain types of terrain can really make a difference if the dog isn't used to it. Strong scents such as certain mints can overwhelm a dog as well and need to be worked through as added insurance. Working over thistles and berry vines is another little annoyance for some dogs that needs to be addressed before entering a test. Going from a hot, dry climate to a damp, cool climate and vice versa can make a difference to some dogs. Take the time to give your dog a wide variety of experiences before you try to enter a TDX test. They are expensive to enter and you may have to travel quite a distance to get to one. It is hard to get into a test as the demand is much greater than the spots available.

AKC TESTS

This brings us to TDX tests and AKC rules pertaining to them. For a TDX test your dog does not have to be certified as they do for a TD. Having passed a TD is all that is required. A dog shall be awarded the TDX title upon having passed a TDX test in which at least two dogs actually participated or at a combined TD/TDX test where at least three dogs participated. You need to refer to Chapter 4 of your AKC Tracking Regulations for specific regulations regarding the TDX. If you are familiar with the regulations on track requirements, you will have a better idea of what to expect on a track and where you will most likely find it, which will help you to be a better handler.

In conclusion, I would like to encourage you to go on into TDX training with your Chesapeake. If training for the TD left you and your dog wanting more of this kind of work, then you are a good candidate to go on to the TDX. A Chesapeake who is motivated to track for you certainly has all the equipment needed to get the job done. Granted, the TDX is more than just a little bit more difficult than the TD, but don't be put off by the small number of Chesapeakes who have accomplished this. The Chesapeake's great nose and perseverance should give the breed many more TDX titles than it currently has.

CHESAPEAKES WITH TDX TITLES

Ch. Wyndham's Algonquin—Helen Szostak	1983
Cub's Bloody Red Baron, CD, WDX—Sally Diess	1985
Ch. Chesareid Ginger, UDTX—Sally Diess	1989
Ch. Nesnah's Shadow B's Mr. Walnut, UDTX, JH, WDX—Stephanie Adelmann	1990

REFERENCES

AKC Tracking Regulations (American Kennel Club, 51 Madison Ave., New York, N.Y. 10010)

Tracking Dog by Glen Johnson (Arner Publications, 1975)

Go Find: Training Your Dog to Track by Wilson Davis (Howell Book House, 1974)

CFTC/CAFTC/AFC Nanuk of Cheslang, with his owner-trainer-handler, Hans Kuch of Canada. Nanuk was a favorite with the crowd.

20

Chesapeakes in Canada

THE CHESAPEAKE BAY duck dog appears to have found its way into western Canada at about the time of the American Civil War. David Rankin wrote from Saskatchewan, "Chesapeakes have been in western Canada since before the railroad's completion in 1885. Canadians have exported Chesapeakes back to the United States, notably George Fairbairn in the 1930s with his Bud Parker dogs from Neepawa, Manitoba. I think that most progressive Canadian breeders have always realized that they had to measure their dogs against the best they could find, rather than remain secure in their own backyard. Consequently, I believe there will always be a steady traffic of brown dogs back and forth across the border between the United States and Canada. That is a necessary and good thing if we are to progress."

Although Mr. Rankin used the affectionate term, common among field trialers who dubbed the Chesapeakes "brown dogs" because they are not black Labradors, the deadgrass color was favored in his part of Canada. Walter Roesler wrote, "When the Chesapeake was introduced into Saskatchewan and Alberta, gunners wanted a lighter color to blend with the light stubble and prevailing light color of the surroundings. Getting this lighter color was only a matter of selection.''

BREED PIONEERS IN CANADA

Back and forth across the border, Americans like Earl Henry and others in Minnesota and North Dakota worked together with Canadian breeders to develop a gun dog to suit their prevailing hunting conditions. Harry Felt was located in Saskatchewan, and L. Caldecott bred Chesapeakes in far western British Columbia. "Traffic" between British Columbia and Washington State was a natural consequence of their common border.

These serious breeders were knowledgeable about conformation and the type of balance needed in a sound working gun dog that must be a superior swimmer, a powerful, athletic individual especially suited for work in severe weather conditions by the protection of the unique breed-typical coat that kept the dog warm and dry throughout a working day. The American Chesapeake Club founded in 1918 recognized the contributions of Canadian breeders, and F. E. Richmond of Calgary, Alberta, assisted Americans Earl Henry and W. H. Orr, in developing the first AKC-approved Standard for the breed.

Later, in the 1930s the American Standard underwent a revision that is only slightly changed today, and Canadian George Fairbairn worked on the committee with John E. Hurst representing a family of Maryland breeders and Anthony A. Bliss of Long Island.

Elizabeth Lavoy started her **Conroy Marsh** kennels in 1945, located at Boulder, Ontario. She was told that there were only nine breeders or kennels in Canada at that time: **Copper City**, owned by William Brennan, Moranda, Quebec; **Oil City**, Frank Cockerel, **Carnmoney**, Munro Coleman, and **Baker's** prefix used by Archie Baker; all three of these were located at Edmonton. **Gilroy** denoted Bob Gilroy, Coquitlan, B.C., and the **Midnapore** kennels of Peg Des Roches were at Vancouver, B.C. Ed Bolander at Edmonton had **Chesaseal** kennels. Leverne Wright of Picton, Ontario, was a breeder known for "Ducklore of Cocoa King," but it seems unlikely that this combination of two well-known American kennel names could actually have been an officially recognized kennel name, even in another country. If anybody is counting, that ninth breeder must have been Mrs. Lavoy herself.

Since that time, a number of new breeders were added. In Ontario: **Waterlord** owned by Don Crompton, Carleton Place; **Watermaster**, Bill Levigne, Weston; **Jojak**, J. & J. Babcock, Sydenham; **Bluteal**, Lionel Adair, Consecon; **Burrits Rapids**, Gim Chadwick, Merrickville, and **Garjo**, Gary and Joan Brown, Slittsville. **Chessyland**, Massey, Ontario ends this list.

Manitoba contributed **Glengarvan**, owned by Gus Stone, and **Peake** used by Cyril Hicks, both of Winnipeg. **Fourte** was the kennel name of Don and Myrna Torrie, Regina, Saskatchewan. More kennels in Alberta were Brian West's **Westpeake** at Sylvan Lake; **Sedgecroft**, belonging to David and Phyllis Rankin of Calgary, and **Redwood** owned by Jim and Mary Anne Kilgannon at Edmonton. Alvin Carlson's **Timberview** appears to have been at Aldergrove, B.C. I am not sure what his connection was with **Carnmoney**; I seem to be dealing with conflicting sources. Rita Street at Victoria, B.C., has used **Garry Oak's** and **Westernoaks** as kennel prefixes. Hans Kuch adopted **Cheslang** for his British Columbia kennel at Half Moon Bay.

MODERN DAY CHESAPEAKES

A few new names appeared in the 1980s. **Mossbank**, used by the MacKinlays at Morpeth, Ontario. **Debwill** kennels is owned by Bill and Deborah LaChanse near Niagara Falls. Both these kennels have been active in shows, and each has been the home of a Best in Show winner. **Riverview**, operated by Dave and Bonnie Joy on Wolfe Island, Ontario, tries to combine the Best in Show and field bloodlines. **Sun Country** is the name adopted by Ted Hay in Saskatchewan. **Beartown** belongs to the Bordos in Ontario. **Karmilen** is a prefix used by Len Pettit in Redwater, Alberta. This is not a complete roster of Canadian kennel names. It is sometimes difficult to distinguish between a prefix identifying all dogs from a given kennel, and a prefix used by one owner only for dogs owned by him/her. Many Canadian dogs, like many in the United States, go on record by winning titles or placements in shows and performance events whose names do not carry any breeder's "handle" by which their background could be identified.

Many American names appear in the records of Canadian events. The first Chesapeake to go Best in Show in Canada or in any country was an American-bred and -owned bitch, Ch. Queen Cocoa, shown in Newfoundland by an American handler in 1974. The first Canadian-bred and -owned Best in Show Chesapeake was Can. Ch. Mossbank Model Chet in 1979 at Montreal. In 1986 Am. & Can. Ch. Neptune's Mullica Mischief, bred in the United States by Eileen Antolino and owned by Bill LaChanse and Jan Thomas, went Best in Show at Credit Valley Kennel Club show at Toronto.

About thirty years ago a Canadian handler was offering a package deal, to show an American dog to a Canadian championship in one trip to Canada. He guaranteed at least one Group placement because this was the only way the dog could be sure of winning in competition, for Chesapeakes were usually not shown in Canadian shows. More Canadians have begun to show their dogs, and Americans now frequently travel to Canada to show their dogs to earn Canadian titles in conformation and in Obedience.

In Field Trials the relationship is even closer, for the Specialty Trials in Canada could not muster enough Canadian Chesapeakes to be held successfully and are dependent on support from the Americans, whose entries are always forthcoming. A Specialty Trial is an old home week, a gathering of the clan, whether in Canada or in the United States, for with their relatively small numbers, the Chesapeake field trialers all know each other very well. It has not been unusual for American Chesapeakes

CFTC/CAFTC Caroway's Captain Ernie, bred by Carol Andersen, and owned by Jack and Jackie Scheels.

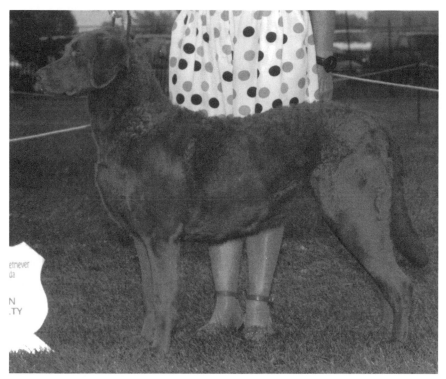

Am. & Can. Ch. Chesabar's Brittany, breeder-owner-handler Patsy Barber. Best of Breed, Chesapeake Bay Retriever Club of Canada National Specialty Show 1992, from the Bred-By-Exhibitor Class. Brittany was Best in Sweepstakes, American Chesapeake Club National Specialty Show 1991.

to earn the Canadian Field Trial titles: Canadian Field Trial Champion and Canadian Amateur Field Trial Champion; Canadian dogs with AKC field championships are quite rare. They are not often campaigned in American all-breed trials, although there are always some Canadians participating in the American Chesapeake Club Specialty Trial.

The Chesapeake Bay Retriever Club of Canada has for some years sponsored booster shows, similar to American Chesapeake Club supported entries, with the aim of increasing Chesapeake entries in the all-breed shows, and especially to put the breed before the public in shows attractive to spectators such as the big benched shows at Toronto. Recently the CBRCC has designated an annual Specialty show, and these have drawn impressive support from American show and Obedience exhibitors.

But it is not only Specialty events that attract the Americans. There is a steady trickle across the border as exhibitors who consider their dogs ready to be shown in Canada select convenient shows and go there for a week or a long weekend. In all its diverse areas, the breed still belongs to both countries.

21

Chesapeakes Abroad

THE CHESAPEAKE BREED is not known to have crossed the Atlantic before 1936. The first Chesapeakes to be exported to England from the United States were brought in by the Earl of Sefton, to improve his Labradors. At that time the Kennel Club registered Interbred Retrievers, which could be bred into one or another of the recognized retriever breeds, and the existence of common ancestry for the Chesapeake Bay Retriever and the English retrievers is well documented.

These first Chesapeakes in England were Ch. Chesacroft Dark Hazard, and some puppies from Chesacroft kennels owned by Anthony A. Bliss. The quarantine was disastrous to the puppies, but the adult dog came through it well. It is not known that he was bred to Chesapeake bitches in England. Dr. Helen Ingleby once mentioned to me that she had bred to Chesacroft Dark Hazard.

Ryshot Yank's Sea Star of Arnac, bred by Margaret Izzard and Janet Horn, became Arnac Kennels' foundation bitch. She was by Ryshot Welcome Yank out of the import Eastern Waters' Ryshot Rose.

CHESAPEAKES IN GREAT BRITAIN

Dr. Ingleby was an English breeder who was a pathologist at a Philadelphia hospital, and during her many years of residence in the United States, she became devoted to the Chesapeake breed, and the dogs she produced were of exceptionally high quality. She named her dogs for American rivers, and did not adopt a formal kennel name. Her bitch, Brandywine, is reported to have gone Best of Breed at Crufts, at about this time in the 1930s. She took a bred bitch into England to whelp a litter in quarantine. As soon as the puppies were weaned, they were permitted to leave the quarantine, and their mother could then be shipped back to the States at her owner's convenience. Dr. Ingleby told of her sister and herself loading the puppies into a car and driving through Scotland selling puppies as they went. One of the purchasers was W. Somerset Maugham. In spite of Dr. Ingleby's attempts to bring the breed she loved into her native land, the dearth of breeding stock remained such that the Chesapeakes she left there were bred to Labradors, and so these early importations failed to establish the breed as a separate one in Britain.

World War II further delayed the exportation of Chesapeakes to Europe, but American servicemen stationed in England brought their dogs with them, and the next introductions of the breed were in this random fashion. It was in the early 1960s that Captain Robert Conlin put his Alpine Abi through quarantine, later bringing the dog home when his tour of duty was ended. Abi sired at least one litter out of a bitch who appears to have been bred in Britain. At about this time, Bruce Kennedy, who bred cattle in Scotland, sent a man to look at cattle on the eastern shore of Maryland, and this emissary's reports of the Chesapeake dogs of that area so intrigued Mr. Kennedy that he commissioned the purchase of a bitch, and named her Doonholme Dusty. Doonholme Dusty flourished in Scotland, and was several times bred to a dog owned by a gamekeeper, Brandy of Cowal by Alpine Abi.

This was the only Chesapeake breeding in Britain when Margaret Izzard of **Ryshot** kennels, best known for excellent Flat-Coated Retrievers, and also for breeding and training Labradors and Goldens, became interested in learning about the Chesapeake at first hand. In 1967 she acquired a puppy from Mr. Kennedy, which she named Ryshot Welcome Yank. She trained him for the field and worked him with her other retrievers. Mrs. Izzard worked her dogs hard, picking up at the shoots on estates, and Yank was always asked for by estates where coastal waters had to be worked. Mrs. Izzard was active in showing her retrievers, which were truly of "dual" character, and her showing of Yank did much to make the Chesapeake known in England. Yank was about a year old when I made his acquaintance and that of Margaret and Dennis Izzard. When Yank was approaching the age of five, we agreed that it was time to seek a suitable mate for him, and from a thoughtfully selected breeding Margaret imported Eastern Waters' Ryshot Rose, who in 1974 produced a litter by Yank. This bitch died not long after. Two of her daughters went to Sweden, and the breeder retained her choice of the bitch puppies, Ryshot Yank's Sea Star. I saw this puppy at the age of seven months, and in the summer of 1975 I mourned with the British dog fancy the passing of Margaret Izzard, whose death was a great loss to the Chesapeake breed as well as to her legion of friends and her devoted husband.

Mr. J. H. A. Allen, who farmed and bred cattle in Devonshire, remembered that when he was a small boy he lived near an American Army base. One of the officers had a Chesapeake of which he and his mother became very fond. Many years later, his love of shooting and dissatisfaction with available Labradors prompted him to obtain a Chesapeake bitch from Mr. Kennedy. Her character and ability so confirmed his feelings for the breed that when illness prevented her being bred, he imported a bitch puppy from America, Eastern Waters' Morag, who produced the second litter sired by Ryshot Welcome Yank in 1975. Some of the puppies from this and from the Izzards' litter were exported to France, Denmark, Sweden and Finland.

When my husband and I visited England at the end of the 1970s, we found Joyce Munday working with Chesapeakes from the Yank-Morag breeding, and Christine Parris enjoying the good fortune of having for her foundation bitch Margaret Izzard's choice for herself, Ryshot Yank's Sea Star.

These breeders, working and showing their Chesapeakes, were doing much to stimulate interest in the breed. Understandably, the English retriever breeds are strongly entrenched in their country of origin, but the greatest obstacle to the establishment and growth of the Chesapeake breed in England appeared to be the quarantine.

Chris Parris, after her marriage to Sir John Spencer-Smith, became better known to the Chesapeake fancy as Lady Spencer-Smith, breeding under the kennel name of **Arnac Bay** and maintaining a connection with Hazelhouse Quarantine kennels, which alleviates the anxieties of importation. Chris, now Mrs. Mayhew, kindly contributed the following updating titled "U.K. History".

> With just two kennels of Chesapeakes operating in 1977, those of Sharland and Arnac, showing and working their dogs on the shoots, interest grew and more fanciers appeared. Sandy Hastings, the wife of a gamekeeper, was one of those first fanciers. Previously having owned Labradors, Sandy bought a bitch puppy, Arnac Bay Abbey, and started her Chesapeake kennel with the kennel name **Chesabay**.
>
> In 1979 a bitch puppy of the same breeding as Abbey was purchased by Janet Morris of Wales. This puppy, Arnac Bay Beck, was to start the **Penrose** Chesapeakes. These new owners and their dogs continued with the Chesapeake tradition by both showing and working their dogs. Abbey was the first Chesapeake to run in a U.K. Field Trial when in 1979 Sandy took the plunge. Janet followed with Beck some two years later, but although working test awards were now being won by Chesapeakes, that elusive Field Trial award was not to come until a later date.
>
> The show ring saw a slight increase in numbers, but no major awards were made to Chesapeakes until 1982 when Chestnut Hills Arnac Drake was released from quarantine and went to his first show, the United Retriever Club, some two weeks later. Drake went Best of Breed and Best Puppy in Breed, and then went on to go Best in Show and Best Puppy in Show from an entry of over three hundred dogs! Chesapeakes were on the map.

240

Am. Ch. Chestnut Hills Arnac Drake, import owned in the U.K. by Christine Spencer-Smith. Shown in the U.S.A. by his breeder Karen Anderson who also handled him to the American Chesapeake Club WD title.

In 1983 a group of Chesapeake owners and enthusiasts, piloted by Joyce Munday, and Christine Spencer-Smith, and Janet Morris, got together at a pub in Newbury, Berkshire, and formed the Chesapeake Bay Retriever Club for U.K. fanciers. The main object of the club being to keep the breed dual purpose and to run shows and working events.

Several new kennels emerged. Richard Playle, a keen wildfowler, started the **Riptide** kennels with a male, Arnac Bay Cool Customer, and later a bitch, Westering Alfalfa. Angela Ingram bred and showed Golden Retrievers at the **Barklands** kennels when she branched out into Chesapeakes with a bitch, Arnac Bay Eventide of Barklands. John and Molly Barker bought a male, Arnac Bay Endurance, who started a love of the breed for the Barkers and the formation of the **Chesepi** kennels, where John would work the dogs and Molly would show them. Westering Brown Sugar of Chesepi became the foundation bitch. Gaynor and Terry Bailey of the **Gunstock** kennels had previously owned and trained for Field Trials most of the native British gun dogs, when they were tempted by the Chesapeake and bought Penrose Brownie of Gunstock.

Arnac Bay Dawnflight of Penrose, the first Chesapeake to win Field Trial awards in the United Kingdom. Owned and handled by Janet Morris and bred by Christine Spencer-Smith.

Breaking New Ground

In 1984, Janet Morris entered a Novice any-variety retriever Field Trial with her second Chesapeake purchase, a sedge bitch, Arnac Bay Dawnflight of Penrose. Dawn broke the Field Trial barrier and was placed third, the first time that a Chesapeake had won a U.K. Field Trial award. Her ecstatic breeder, Christine Spencer-Smith, was there watching and a photograph and article of the historic moment made the pages of the *Shooting Times*. This was the best advertisement for the breed we could have had.

The same year a Chesapeake made history in another aspect of dog work when Sharland Coxswain and his owner Alan Cox broke the ranks of the Working Trials to win a PD (puppy dog) stake normally not open to civilian handlers. Coxswain was bred by Joyce Munday. The Chesapeake's versatility was proven with this, as yet, unbeaten achievement.

The newly formed club held its first show the year after its inception, and Millie Buchholz from the United States was invited to judge. A record number of Chesapeakes arrived for the show and for Working

242

tests (similar to the American WD program) the following day. Bruce Gauntlett's young female, Penrose Bronwen, was Best in Show, and her father, Chestnut Hills Arnac Drake, Best Opposite Sex.

In 1985, two more Chesapeakes joined the ranks of those with Field Trial awards, namely Dawn's sister, Delta, bred, owned and handled by Christine Spencer-Smith, and Penrose Brownie of Gunstock, bred by Janet Morris and owned and handled by Gaynor Bailey. Dawn herself won several more awards in Janet's capable hands. The club show for that year saw Janet's Arnac Bay Beck of Penrose win Best in Show.

It was time for the boys in 1986, and a full brother to Dawn and Delta, Arnac Bay Endurance, was handled by his owner John Barker to be the first male Chesapeake to win a Field Trial award. The club show again had a U.S. breeder to judge, Karen Anderson, who gave Best in Show to Angela Ingram's Arnac Bay Eventide of Barklands.

By this time the prowess of the breed as a working dog was being taken seriously by those Labrador and Golden "diehards," and teams of Chesapeakes were being asked to compete in interbreed competitions and in demonstrations. The early days usually consisted of Janet, Christine, John and Gaynor with their respective Field Trial dogs, but more were to follow. A great honor for the breed was the invitation given to Janet and Dawn to compete in a demonstration Working test at the Game Fair, the largest country show for the shooting fraternity. The following year both Gaynor and Janet worked Chesapeakes.

Registrations for puppies at the Kennel Club climbed from zero in 1979 to sixty-two in 1987, the emphasis still being on dual purpose or "working only" homes.

Penrose Delaware Dimbat of Tyheolog won the Club's show in 1987 for his owner, Elaine Griffin, an Irish Water Spaniel breeder, who had decided to try a Chesapeake.

Two more dogs gained Field Trial awards in 1988, both sons of Endurance. They were the Barkers' own home-bred Chesepi Amigo Mio, handled by John, and another home-bred dog, Janet Morris's Penrose Eclipse. The club show was won for the first time by a Field Trial award winner, Christine Spencer-Smith's Arnac Bay Delta.

Penrose produced two more Field Trial award winners in 1989 with Janet's own Penrose Gale Force and Brian Campling's Penrose Fullflood Gamescout. Westering Brown Sugar won several awards for John Barker and a new face appeared, Linda Partridge with Chesabay Coral of Braidenvale. This turned out to be the duo to watch. Linda, a gamekeeper's wife, had previously owned and bred Dobermanns. With the purchase of Coral, and a determination to succeed in Field Trials, Linda sought professional guidance. The right dog, the right person and a lot of work produced the breakthrough for the breed. Linda and Coral *won* a Novice any-variety retriever trial! The Chesapeake was second to no one! For ten years the breed had battled against the dominance of the Labrador and the Golden, but this was success itself and history for Linda and Coral, as well as a feather in the cap for Coral's breeder, Sandy Hastings.

The dual purpose quest also showed its success when for the second year in a row the Best in Show at the club show was a Field Trial award winner, the Barkers' Chesepi Amigo Mio. It was the year, 1990, when Crufts dog show finally gave Chesapeakes their own classes instead of the normal routine when they were grouped with other "rare" breeds under Any Variety Not Separately Classified (AVNSC), otherwise known among exhibitors in these groups as "Any variety not seriously considered!" The Chesapeakes were on their own at last, and Chesepi Amigo Mio made it a double by going Best of Breed at Crufts. Arnac Bay Delta won through from the Field Trial class to go Best Opposite.

It was a truly international club show in 1990, with Catharina Lindstrom of Sweden judging and Best in Show and Best Opposite going to U.S. imports, namely Christine's Chestnut Hills Arnac Wye Oak and Jane Smith's Berteleda Westering Sequio.

Christine Spencer-Smith had the honor of judging the breed at Crufts in 1991, the show's centenary year, and gave Best of Breed to Janet Morris's Penrose Jamaica Rum, with Jane Smith's Caroway's Westerin' Geronimo as Best Opposite. Christine's own female, Chesabay Crystal of Arnac, won the club's show, and like Amigo before her, did the double by winning Crufts in January 1992. A young male, Braidenvale Arowak, bred and owned by Linda Partridge from her first Chesapeake litter, went Best Opposite.

This show success for Linda was, however, overshadowed by the greatest win to date for the U.K. Chesapeake. Linda and Coral (a litter sister to the Crufts winner) entered an Open Field Trial—and won! Unless you have a knowledge of the difficulty and standard of the British Field Trials, you cannot imagine what a success story this was. Every true Chesapeake enthusiast was ecstatic. This dog and handler were poetry in motion, the communication between them was enviable to all gun-dog handlers.

The club show was won by Christine Spencer-Smith's Arnac Bay Jetsam, who like his mother before him won Crufts at the January 1993 show. Best Opposite was Angela Ingram's Chesendure Sea Breeze of Barklands.

Continued Success

Chesapeakes continue to gain strength in the U.K., their working abilities now taken as a serious threat to the popularity of the other breeds, in particular with the wildfowl hunter who has realized that this breed has everything that is required. The main kennels have continued to breed, show and work their dogs and have been joined in recent years by Brian Campling with **Gamescout** kennels and Linda Partridge with **Braidenvale**, both keen working competitors. There are more Chesapeakes being worked in Field Trials and tests, and even more working "picking up" on the organized shoots that often have bags of two hundred to five hundred birds a day.

New admirers are gained mainly from those who are interested in the dog's working capabilities, and this is a factor that has remained in the minds of the U.K. breeders. The numbers of dogs being shown has remained small and very rarely does a Chesapeake win a major award at all-breed shows. The U.K. breeders consider this a good trend and jealously guard the working aspect of the breed while trying to produce a good-looking dog at the same time.

PROGRESS IN FRANCE

France is the next country into which comparatively early importations of Chesapeakes are known to have been made. The Comte de Bonvouloir, a breeder of Golden Retrievers, and founder and first president of the Retriever Club de France, began to introduce Chesapeakes from the United States shortly after World War II. The first to be recorded were a bitch, Cinnamon of Whichway, bred by Mrs. W. Huntting Howell, and a dog, Lucky Boy of Tesuque, bred by Peter Beasley. There were other importations within the next few years, and Mrs. A. W. Owens, Jr., was one of the breeders who sent Chesapeakes to France in the late 1940s.

On a visit to New York City, the Comte attended the Westminster Kennel Club show and was welcomed by the few of us who exhibited retriever breeds there. At this time the Comte had over thirty Goldens in his kennel, Le Chenil de Saint-Jean-du-Bois (the Kennel of Saint John of the Wood), and he showed to their championships the first Goldens to attain that title in France. The Comte J. de Bonvouloir was the author of a delightful book, *Les Retrievers et Leur Dressage*, now many years out

M. Philippe Valette has owned and hunted over Chesapeakes in France for more than 40 years.

of print, but well worth a search to possess it. It includes a chapter on the origin and description of the Chesapeake Bay Dog Retriever and is illustrated with charming line drawings: The coy flirtation between the Chesapeake and her legendary suitor, the otter, is a gem.

Although the Chenil de Saint-Jean-du-Bois is no more, there are still a few Chesapeakes in France that carry on its bloodlines bred with more recent imports. M. Philippe Valette, an ardent duck hunter who has owned this breed for some forty years, had his first one from the Comte de Bonvouloir's last litter. He imported dogs in the late 1950s and early 1960s from Alpine kennels and from Silverdart kennels in the United States. In shoots on his estate, M. Valette and his friends would bring down as many as five hundred ducks in a day, and he found that the other retrievers quit when they get tired, but the Chesapeake keeps on working until the last bird has been retrieved.

The few Chesapeakes in France are used for hunting, and are highly prized by their owners, but little known to the general public. There are many fine hunting breeds of French origin, unknown to most of us outside that country.

This kind of hunting is limited to private estates, and the retriever interest in France has been small, though its formal guardian, the Retriever Club de France, continues, designating its Specialty at the Paris show and holding at least one formal Field Trial a year. *A win at Paris and a "Mention Très Honnorable" in a Field Trial are among the requirements for a retriever to earn a French championship*, so it is essential that a trial be held to provide opportunity for retrievers to prove themselves in the field.

Labradors, easily imported from England, came to outnumber the Goldens in France, and few French retriever owners had ever seen a Chesapeake, when in 1975 my husband and I were temporary residents and exhibited our American champions Eastern Waters' Skipjack, CD, and Eastern Waters' Stardust in a number of dog shows, and attended Field Trials. Our Chesapeakes attracted a great deal of attention and interest. From the litter produced by them while overseas, one bitch remained in France to be trained and hunted by her owner.

Since then, interest in the Chesapeake breed has grown and several have been imported over the years, from the United States and Britain as well as from the Netherlands and Denmark. M. Jean-Louis Pigal reported two Chesapeakes placing in Field Trials in 1992, remarking "the way is now open in France for new good-working Chessies, and with the presence of about six young new dogs for next year (English and Danish lines) we hope that Chesapeake Bay Retrievers will be considered otherwise than just a curiosity."

HOLLAND

Importations into Holland and Denmark have been more recent, but in these watery countries the breed found such favor that its population rapidly increased. Meager information on Holland has been available; the man who first imported Chesapeakes into Holland thought that about nine of the breed had been imported from abroad, first from the United States in the early 1950s, then from the Comte de Bonvouloir in France, from Bruce Kennedy in Scotland and again from the States.

Some of the American breeders known to have exported Chesapeakes to Holland in those early days were Dr. John Lundy, Richard and

Chattahoochee av Komsalo. Best of Breed, Danish Chesapeake Specialty Show 1984 under Millie Buchholz, U.S. Bred by Gun Holmström, Finland, owned by Niels Lind Pederson, Denmark.

Sheila DiVaccaro and Ernest Wermerskirchen. Further American imports in the 1970s were Eastern Waters' Magic Pearl, and a male puppy from Mrs. Robert G. Lee. Chesapeakes bred in Holland have been exported to other European countries including France and Denmark.

In 1971 a Chesapeake club was formed in Holland to promote and safeguard the interests of the breed, and some informal trials were held, but there appears to have been little interest among Dutch Chesapeake owners in participation in Field Trials and shows. The population was reported in the 1970s to be about forty or fifty, and maintains at these figures to the present day, while only occasional breeding takes place.

DENMARK

It is said that the first Chesapeakes to reach Denmark were imported in the late 1930s. However, none of this breeding survived World War

II, and no details have been available. The Chesapeakes that formed the foundation of breeding stock for present-day Denmark were imported from the United States in the mid-1960s: Baronland's Cub's Cary Grant, Sal of Wermerskirchen and some others not fully identified. More were imported continuously, from Holland, Scotland, from Mount Joy kennels and from Smart's kennels among others in the United States and from neighboring Sweden.

In the 1970s, Mr. Ole Lind Pedersen served in several capacities in the Danish Retriever Club, among them as breeding warden for Chesapeakes. The Danish Retriever Club holds Specialty Shows and several Field Trials a year, and a Field Trial award is required for a retriever to earn the title of champion. Mr. Pedersen owned and worked both Chesapeakes and Labradors, using them mostly for hunting and picking up; he has been active in field and show competition, and has done some breeding.

Some breeding also was done at the Dienesmindes kennels of Dan Madsen. Denmark is typical wetland with a very long shoreline, located in the center of the flyway of different ducks and geese, and the hunting is very good, and sometimes great. Upland game is good, too, with no bag limits, for all hunting is on private lands that must be owned or leased by the hunter. The last quarter of this century brings the same changes that have been seen in North America; draining the wetlands deprives the waterfowl of natural habitat and breeding grounds, and this type of hunting becomes a threatened sport in Denmark, too.

Regardless of changes in the sport that developed the breed, the Chesapeake continues to develop a very special group of devotees in its own country and so it is in Denmark, where a nucleus of serious fanciers is working in the breed's interest. The estimated population was one hundred in 1976, when I had the honor of judging an informal Specialty Show. I also had the pleasure of watching a Field Trial held on an estate that was said to have belonged in the Middle Ages to Erik the Red. The population is now reported to have doubled and to number about 200 Chesapeakes at the present time.

Leif Holm succeeded Ole Lind Pedersen as warden and he visited the United States in the 1980s. The following report on Denmark today was sent to me by Birgitte Jorgensen, who says, "in Europe, the Danish Chessie population of about two hundred is outnumbered only by the British one, and since we are a much smaller country, the breed has done fairly well here, although, I guess, we shall for a long time to come still be fighting with the curlies and tollers to avoid being the least popular of the retriever breeds."

Denmark has seen fourteen show champions and one Obedience champion since the first Chesapeake litter was born in 1967. *In Denmark, a retriever must not only qualify in the field before earning a show championship title but must also be over two years old when winning the last show points.*

Most Danish Chesapeakes are still owned by professional or amateur hunters, of whom only a few bother to compete in Field Trials. Several dogs are excelling in Tracking, especially in tracking wounded deer for which an official register of qualified dogs is maintained. Tracking in the Scandinavian countries and in Germany means tracking a blood trail for wounded game, whereas in the U.S. and Canada we earn Tracking titles by following a human foot and body scent.

Of the show champions in Denmark, six have also achieved the international championship: Int. & Dk. Ch. LCh. Marco, bred by J. Marcher, owned by Jorgen Scharff, a good ambassador for the breed because he has been successfully shown in several European countries; Int. & Dk. Ch. Rikke, bred by Frits B. Jensen, owned by Birthe Jeppesen, a sedge bitch with exceptional coat and conformation who came forward from the Veteran class to take Best of Breed under Millie Buchholz in the 1991 Specialty; Int. & Dk. Ch. OTCH World Ch. 89 & 91 Roneklint's Bolette, a showy brown bitch who has proved the breed's versatility by taking several first places in Show, FT, Obedience, Agility and Tracking, and also by being the mother and grandmother of equally capable dogs (The Jorgensens are especially proud of her OTCH because it was achieved in 1987 before any of the recent U.S. and Canadian Obedience Trial Champions made their titles, and they were told that a Chesapeake couldn't do this—Bolette was at that time the fifth youngest Danish dog ever to become an OTCH at just over two years old); Int. & Dk. Ch. Cheslabben Unika Chesbo, WD, bred by B. Jorgensen, owned by B. Ronnow and G. Mortensen; Int. & Dk. Ch. VDHCh. DCh. Cheslabben Bravo Chesbo, WD, a full brother to Unika, bred and owned by Birgitte Jorgensen, whose numerous wins throughout Europe include a Group second at Austria's largest international show, and to the best of his owner's knowledge, he was the first Chesapeake to become a German champion; Int. & Dk. Ch. NLCh. Skyttekonen's Annabel, bred by B. Jeppesen, owned by Jens and Vibeke Jensen, a brown bitch with excellent coat, the holder of numerous European titles.

Birgitte edits the Danish breed book, which contains all available information including breeding statistics, breed history, hip and eye results (there are breeding restrictions on dogs with eye and hip problems that are considered to be hereditary) and so on.

Int. & Dk. Ch. Rikke, nine years old, Best of Breed, Danish Chesapeake Specialty Show 1991, under Millie Buchholz. Rikke is owned by Birthe Jeppesen.

NORWAY AND SWEDEN

In the early 1970s Chesapeakes began to find their way into Norway and Sweden from Denmark, the United States and England. The first Chesapeake in Sweden was Chesachobee's Echo, imported from Mildred Buchholz in 1973 by Josta Westerlund and Lars Andersson. Echo produced the first litter of Chesapeakes in Sweden, in October 1975, sired by one of the first of the breed in Norway, Smarts Petter, owned by Britt Eli Overeng. All dogs entering these two Scandinavian countries are required to spend several months in quarantine, with the exception of those coming from England, which has contributed two Ryshot-bred bitches, brought as puppies from Margaret Izzard's kennel by Marianne Nilsson and Klas Norrman at the New Year of 1975. Once inside one of these countries, a dog may not leave without going through quarantine upon returning. The ramifications surrounding an attempt to breed outside the country, by artificial insemination, are mind-boggling. Dogs may pass freely from Norway to Sweden for breeding, shows and trials.

A quarantine was in force when Gun Holmström imported the first

Chesapeakes into Finland in 1976; two puppies from the first litter bred in Switzerland and the male puppy Eastern Waters' Jeremysquam went from the Finnish quarantine into Sweden. Before his premature death, Jeremysquam sired a litter out of Chesachobee's Echo. Eastern Waters' Winnepesaukee remained in Finland, others followed and in 1978 she produced the first Chesapeake litter in Finland, sired by Chutney. Chewonki, from the first Swedish litter, sired several litters out of Ryshot Yank's Sea Coral, owned by Marianne Nilsson, and registered in her "Vättlestugan" kennel name.

At this time the fanciers in Sweden, Norway and Finland could work closely together to improve and establish the breed and to advance its interests. Specialty events were well and enthusiastically attended, and the leading breeders were experienced with other breeds, and knew how to make use of shows and trials to balance emphasis on type and working ability. Finland was withdrawn from this close and exclusive association when the discovery of rabies in that country in the late 1980s made the quarantine useless and unnecessary, and the Finns opened their borders to the importation of dogs and other livestock. Breeders have kept up their ties and old friendships and remain in communication throughout these three countries and Denmark, and they look to Britain and the United States for new stock and new developments in the breed.

My husband and I brought back very special memories from a trip to Scandinavia in 1979, where he judged a Chesapeake Specialty show in Denmark, followed by the Chesapeake Specialty in Sweden at the time of the midsummer celebrations at Dalarna. The only thing that made it not quite perfect was that when we swam with Chesapeakes and Flat-Coats in a Swedish lake, we could not have our own Chesapeakes with us.

In 1980 the fanciers in Sweden had gained sufficient strength and numbers to start their own Chesapeake Bay Retrieverklubb. It had forty-six members, and in 1981 almost doubled its membership, counting seventy-one members. Once a year the club arranged a Chesapeake Specialty with Show, Field Trial, retriever test and Obedience Trial. This was the pattern of the Specialty event that had been so enjoyed by my husband and me. The club published a newsletter, held field training courses and in 1986 included a Tracking trial at its Specialty. At this time there were over one hundred members. With membership dropping back to about seventy, in 1990 the Swedish Chesapeakes joined in the Norwegian Specialty, and other activities were curtailed. Plans made in 1992 call for the Swedish Specialty to be restored as an annual event, and to include field training.

Dual Performance Dogs

Int. Swed. & Nord. Ch. Chewonki was used quite a lot at stud and his most famous offspring were from his four litters with Int. Nord. Ch. Ryshot Yank's Sea Coral, owned by Marianne Nilsson Johansson. The Nordic title was given to a dog earning national championships in Sweden, Norway and Finland in the days when the three countries were locked together in quarantine. It is not impossible to achieve it today, but the quarantine is a strong deterrent. Nord. AFC Int. Nord. Ch. Vättlestugans Nanna, owned by Kjell Svenningsson, was outstanding in Field Trials for many years. Her younger brother Swed. & Nord. AFC Nord. Ch. Vättlestugans Cupido, owned by Catharina and Kaj Lindstrom, died very young and could not fulfill the promise he showed in trials, especially in handling to blind retrieves.

Cupido was bred twice to the lovely bitch Baptist Corner Chobee Judy. Judy was a litter sister to my Ch. Baptist Corner Yankee Spice, CD. Cupido's granddaughter AFC Swed. Ch. Vättlestugans Karelia, owned by Staffan Birkegard, is a recent Field Champion, making the title in 1990. Also worth mentioning as a trial dog is Swed. Ch. Westering Arrival, owned by the Lindstroms. She did very well in the few trials she competed in; sadly she died at the age of five. She was bred once and her natural ability has gone through to her offspring. In 1991 excellent performance in trials are reported for Swed. Ch. Double Coat's a Hard Days Night, WDX, bred and owned by the Lindstroms, Swed. Ch. Vättlestugans Nienna, owned by Staffan Birkegard, and Lena Ahls' Uved's Peppergrass.

In 1979, Int. Swed. & Nord. SF Ch. Ryshot Yank's Sea Coral, and her daughter Swed. & Nordic SF Ch. Vättlestugans Hera were the only Swedish show champions. Hera made the International Championship in 1980. Since then, twenty-two Swedish Chesapeakes have made at least one championship title, in either Norway or Sweden, and many have titled in both.

There have been three Field Trial Champions, which were also dual champions since they had both Field and Show titles. First was Vättlestugans Nanna in 1980. Vättlestugans Cupido titled in 1982, and Vättlestugans Karelia in 1990.

Every year the dogs with a "first" in Eliteclass can enter a Mastership Trial for retrievers. Vättlestugans Nanna qualified for several years and placed high at most of them. In 1986, Nanna won an international Field Trial (arranged in Sweden once a year) and got CACIT. She had a reserve CACIT before.

Goose Hunters in Sweden: Emma and Bryn, owned by Catharina and Kaj Lindstrom.

A Mastership Tracking trial is held once a year for the most qualified dogs (all breeds) in Sweden. In 1991 a Chesapeake became Master of the year: Vättlestugans Haugtussa, owned by Walde Dahlstrand.

There is one Swedish Obedience Trial Champion: Masens Shawondasi, owned by Elon Hallgren.

A total of 258 Chesapeakes have been born or have come to live in Sweden since 1973. There are about one or two litters born per year, and for the moment there are about 120 Chesapeakes in the country. Swedish fanciers hope for the future that the borders to the rest of the world, not only to rabies-clear countries, will be opened to allow them to travel with and import dogs more easily. The Chesapeake breed has supporters in Sweden and is an established breed that has come to stay.

In attempting to trace Chesapeake progress in Sweden from 1979 to the present, I am indebted to Marianne Johansson, and to Catharina Lindstrom, for the informative reports that I have pieced together to form the basis for the above extended account of Chesapeakes in Sweden.

Int. Swed. & Nor. Ch. Penrose Cherokee Chief, WDX. Bred in Wales by Janet Morris, and owned in Sweden by Catharina and Kaj Lindstrom.

FINLAND

Gun Holmström's account of Chesapeakes in Finland begins with her Eastern Waters' Winnepesaukee, by Am. & Can. Ch. Eastern Waters' Skipjack, CD, ex Am. & Ch. Eastern Waters' Stardust, bred by Janet Horn. "Winne" gained her title Finnish Champion in 1981. Later Chesapeakes have been imported from Sweden, Norway, Denmark, Great Britain and the U.S. In 1981 the Chesapeake Club was founded with Gun Holmström as chairperson. The club publishes a magazine four times a year and holds a yearly summer weekend for the members. The training for Field Trials and the club show are most popular and never can you see so many Chesapeakes elsewhere in this country at the same time.

A total of eighty-nine Chesapeakes have been registered by the Finnish Kennel Club at the end of 1992. Quite a few of these have been exported to other countries. Except for the "Komsalo"-bred dogs, the "High Noons" and the "Olalis" have bred two litters each.

When it comes to health problems, there have been some progressive retinal atrophy (PRA) and Hip Dysplasia cases, but not more than seem to be the average for the breed. Since the quarantine border has been set between Finland and Sweden/Norway, the exchange of breeding material

Vättlestugans Venus, bred by Marianne Johansson in Sweden, and owned by Anita Soinjoki, Finland.

has stopped, but on the other hand the Finns can now move freely in the rest of the world with their dogs.

Quite a few International Champions and many Finnish Champions have been made up and showing has been popular. Some dogs have earned Field Trial awards but most are used for shooting and wildfowling. A few litters are planned for the next years but here we prefer to "hurry slowly."

SWITZERLAND

"The show at Bern, Switzerland, in April 1975 was the first European show in which my husband and I exhibited the two Chesapeakes that had come with us to live in Europe for a time determined by my

Three generations owned by Gun Holmström: 1) Finn. Ch. Eastern Waters' Winnepesaukee (left), 2) Int. & Finn. Ch. Frideborg av Komsalo (right), 3) Int. & Finn. Ch. Filippa av Komsalo (middle).

Gorgeous Goose av Komsalo, a multiple Best in Show winner at Chesapeake shows in Finland. Bred by Gun Holmström and owned by Eeva Pelttari.

257

husband's assignment to the World Health Organization in Geneva. Like all the shows we went to in Europe, this one was benched, and so there were many interested spectators, and among them was Maya Mächler, who has written the following account of Chesapeakes in Switzerland.

"Before 1975, I found only one Chesapeake living in Switzerland. A Swiss lady took him back to Switzerland after a couple of years when she lived in the United States. He loved to fish in the neighbors' fish pond and it took them a long time to find out who was the thief. . . .

"In 1975, Janet P. Horn and her husband, Dr. Daniel Horn, came to Europe and lived in Gex, France, very near to the Swiss border. They had two of their Chessies with them, Ch. Eastern Waters' Skipjack and Ch. Eastern Waters' Stardust. They showed Skipjack and Dusty, and this was the way I saw the first Chessies and fell in love with them.

"On November 28, 1975, a litter was whelped by Skipjack ex Dusty and got Swiss pedigrees by special permission of the Swiss Springer Spaniel and Retriever Club (today Retriever Club Switzerland). The puppies were born and grew up at Geo Wettstein's place, who is a Golden breeder and made some new experiences, of which she still speaks today!

"Unfortunately, none of the four pups got a place in Switzerland; they went to France and Scandinavia. One of the two that went to France was later brought to the United States by her American owner, Ranee Nevels."

Swiss Breeding Foundations

"In 1976 two dogs were imported to Switzerland: Eastern Waters' Mountaineer and Eastern Waters' Jupiter. Mounty came to the home of Peter and Madeleine Winkler, both excellent trainers. Mounty passed a lot of tests: Companion Dog, Schutzhund I, II and III, International I, II and III, catastrophe (rescue) dog and catastrophe dog in the Swiss Army with Peter, while Madeleine presented him in Sanitary Dog I, II and III.

"Jupiter, imported by Nelly Mauler of Auvernier, became my dog in the spring of 1978. I was an absolute greenhorn in training and showing, but Jupiter did very high pointed CDs. He went on to be Swiss Champion, Winner of the European Pokal 1978 (Switzerland/Germany/France); World Champion 1979 and World Champion 1981. He is the Adam of the Swiss Chesapeake breeding. I loved Jupiter so very much, and because of his quality I decided to get him a female. Eastern Waters' Juno joined us in the spring of 1979. She's the Eve of the Swiss breeding.

"Juno did CD and she was very soon a Swiss Champion. Both of them, Jupiter and Juno, were at many shows and earned large numbers of CACs and CACIBs.

"Juno had three litters: 1981 and 1983 by Jupiter, 1985 by Lord (France), whose dam was an Eastern Waters bitch, too. Lord's owner, M. Philippe Valette, France, has owned Chesapeakes for forty years but still says that Lord has been his best dog. Lord had been bred in the Netherlands. He was a hardworking hunting dog.

"Juno's daughter of her 1983 litter, Swiss and Int. Ch. Water-Lovers Charming-Angie, has had three litters: 1987 and 1989 by Swiss Ch. Water-Lovers Sunset-Spikey, her half-brother, and 1991 by Swiss Ch. Gunstock Brown Bosun, owned by Audrey Austin of the United States, living in Germany. Angie won a lot of CACs and CACIBs, she is a Swiss CD, she placed in a Field Novice class and has two excellents in Search Dog Tests and the Special Medal of Swiss Cynological Society in Tracking. Spikey is a Swiss CD and he got the Special Medals in Search *and* Tracking, and at his first two Field Trials he took a first and a third in Novice and placed in Open.

"Angie's daughter Swiss Ch. Water-Lovers Nashville Judy, whelped in 1987, had two litters: 1990 by Swiss Ch. Gunstock Brown Bosun, and 1992 by Water-Lovers Chattanooga Charly, a litter brother of her dam Angie. Charley is a Swiss CD and Schutzhund I and was, after Mounty, the second Chesapeake to serve the Swiss Army as catastrophe dog, and the Swiss Army is the place where the dog gets paid better than the owner/trainer/handler! (We have a militia system). Actually I own Angie, Spikey, Judy and a female puppy by Charly ex Judy, named Water-Lovers Maximum. Maxie was Youth champion and Best of Breed from the Youth class at the International Show of Bern, 1993.

"To my knowledge, we have at this time thirty-two Chesapeakes in Switzerland, of which twenty-five are 'Water-Lovers' whelped here. To date, we are lucky to have only two cases of stationary cataract, which will never bother the dog or affect sight. No PRA; I keep my fingers crossed! Only two dogs had bad hips, both were put down.

"Water-Lovers Nessy, litter brother to Judy, has been so well trained by his owner Claudia Wyser that he is a member of the Official Swiss Rescue Team (catastrophes). The team of Nessy and Claudia was a member of the Swiss Rescue Team that went to save people at the terrible earthquake in Turkey in 1992, at Erzincan.

"In 1989, for the first time, a Chesapeake won the Swiss Retriever Club Show and went Best in Show: Swiss Ch. Water-Lovers Hilly-Billie, CD, whelped 1981, owned by Hedi Niedermann. The win was repeated the next year, 1990, when Swiss Ch. Gunstock Brown Bosun went Best in Show, with his first owner, J.-J. de Rham.

"Nine Chesapeakes have finished the Swiss Champion title. Ch.

Swiss Ch. Water-Lovers Hilly-Billie, CD, Best in Show, Retriever Club of Switzerland Specialty 1989 for all retriever breeds. "Billie" was bred by Maya Mächler, and owned, trained and handled by Mrs. H. Niedermann.

Water-Lovers Sunny-Jerry, owned by Anna Sagesser, is also German Champion, CD, Sanitary Dog I, II and III and has the Special Medal for Tracking. Ch. Water-Lovers Nebraska Sammy, owned by Josef Waltisberg, is World Champion 1992. Nine additional Chesapeakes have been imported into Switzerland since 1980, from the United States, Canada, Great Britain, Denmark and France."

Toward the Future

"For the future of the Chesapeake in Switzerland, in breeding there will probably be one litter a year for the next three years. In working, one is a hunting dog, but it clearly looks as though rescue work is the future; several dogs are trained for Sanitary, Catastrophe, Avalanche, Search and Tracking tests. Three to five, approximately, will do some Field Trials. Two are trained for Agility.

"I try to keep Eastern Waters in my breeding and am very glad that for fifteen years I can count on Janet Horn for helpful advice. Who else should a greenhorn breeder be able to ask and trust, if it isn't the person

260

who bred her/his first dogs? Here in Switzerland, one can feel very 'lonesome' as, up to today still, the lone Chesapeake breeder.''

GERMANY

Since Audrey Austin accompanied her husband, Gene, to his station in Germany she has become deeply involved in the Chesapeake breed, and has contributed the following report on Chesapeakes in Germany.

"Chesapeakes are a rare and exotic breed in Germany. Until early 1993, there have been only two litters bred here. The others have been imported.

"German, Swiss, Luxembourg Champion Gunstock Brown Bosun, owned by Audrey Austin in the show ring, and Holiday Surprise, owned by Karen Von Low on the field scene, have made Chesapeake friends all across Germany.

"Bred in England at Gunstock kennels, Bosun came to Germany via Switzerland in 1990. He finished his German Championship with five Best of Breed wins, including the World Dog Show in Dortmund and the

German, Swiss, Luxembourg Champion Gunstock Brown Bosun, owned by Audrey Austin. Bosun went Best in Show, Swiss Retriever Club Specialty Show 1990, over all retriever breeds. He was bred in Great Britain by Mr. and Mrs. T. K. Bailey.

Holiday Suprise, owned by Karen von Low, retrieving in a German Hunt Test where she won a second place.

title of World Champion 1991. In Switzerland, his career included Best in Show, Group third and five Best of Breeds.

"Holiday Surprise (Holly), an American import, has completed eight different tests and trials all with honors. Hunting Trials in Germany include test in marking, blinds, trailing, retrieving birds and rabbits and tracking the blood trail of deer. In 1991, Holly won the award for Best Hunting Dog in Bavaria, competing against all hunting breeds.

"Together Holly and Bosun produced ten puppies in 1992, about doubling the number of Chesapeakes nationwide. They are now making their debuts and winning in the Show ring, Field and Obedience Trials. The German public is discovering the unique attributes of the Chesapeake with these goodwill ambassadors."

ITALY

The most recent country in Europe to welcome the Chesapeake as a resident breed appears to be Italy. Years ago when my husband and I

The only Chesapeakes in Italy: Rockrun's Fabulous Jessie, and Rockrun's Good Joss, owned by Benedetta Gilardini.

showed our Chesapeakes in different countries we were impressed with the beauty and efficiency of Italian shows, and at that time ours were the only Chesapeakes being shown in Italy. Pleasant associations are awakened by the following from Benedetta Gilardini.

"I fell in love with a Chessie I saw in a magazine when I was living in New York in 1987. After some months I was the proud and happy owner of Rockrun's Good Joss. When we moved back to Italy in 1989, Joss came with us, and has in the meantime been joined by Rockrun's Fabulous Jessie. They are two marvelous dogs! Joss became an Italian Champion in six months. Jessie is very active in Field Trials and is starting on her Obedience.

"As a member of the Italian Retrievers Club, I am very active in promoting our breed. Chesapeakes are wonderful companions, both in the country where I go with them every weekend, as well as in Milan, where I live during the week. And I am very proud when people ask information about them even if some have difficulty in pronouncing the breed's name!"

Benedetta had never thought of showing Joss until Beppe Benelli, the founder of the Italian Retrievers Club convinced her to go to a club show in October 1989, and she enjoyed it so much that she kept showing him until someone told her that he probably was a champion already. The only time another Chesapeake was present was at the Verona International Show in 1989, and Joss went Best of Breed. Joss is now working toward field qualification for the International Championship.

The International Championship is awarded by the FCI (Fédération Cynologique Internationale) on the basis of qualifications in member countries, which include the continent of Europe, as well as Mexico and South American countries. We found there to be a one-year interval required between the first and last awards of the Certificate of Aptitude for International Championship: These awards are to be four CACIBs, which must be won in three different countries, plus a field qualification for retrievers and other hunting breeds. From 1975 to 1976, Am. Ch. Eastern Waters' Skipjack, CD, won nine CACIBs in four countries and added Canadian titles after his return to America. During this period Am. Ch. Eastern Waters' Stardust, shown in fewer shows, won five CACIBs in three countries. Retriever interest shows growth and progress in Western Europe, where retriever field trials seem generally to be modeled closely after English counterparts, and they differ very much from American trials. They also vary from one country to another, and little or no water work may be required in Western Europe, while in Scandinavia the water work is often quite demanding.

As in America, the fame of the Chesapeake has spread because of the breed's prowess in the hunting field, and popularity increases as the Chesapeake becomes more widely known for its unique breed character. The breed character and personality is the source of the devotion and loyalty of fanciers to a degree found in few other breeds. It is casting the same spell over owners overseas and creating a coterie of devotees fully as ardent as those in America. Most of the Europeans who have acquired Chesapeakes and undertaken to carry on with breeding them have or have had other retriever breeds.

Not all new owners are Nimrods; some with a love of the water and outdoor living have liked the Chesapeake as companion, guardian and playmate for the family—another area at which this "specialist" breed excels. In every country the breeders and fanciers who are in a position to be most influential recognize the special qualities of the Chesapeake, and while endeavoring to advance interest, they are alert to the dangers of overbreeding and overpopularity, and a primary aim is to ensure that the breed shall continue in good hands. The Chesapeake in Europe shares the owner's home and is regarded as a member of the family, much loved and highly prized.

Glossary

AFC	Amateur Field Champion
AKC	The American Kennel Club, 51 Madison Avenue, New York, N.Y. 10010
CAFTC	Canadian Amateur Field Trial Champion
CD	Companion Dog—Obedience Title
CDX	Companion Dog Excellent—Obedience Title
CERF	The Canine Eye Registration Foundation, Inc. a nonprofit organization that issues a certificate to clear-eyed dogs after examination by a veterinary ophthalmologist. Purdue University, South Campus Courts, Building A, West Lafayette, Ind. 47907
CFTC or Can. FTC	Canadian Field Trial Champion
CGC	Canine Good Citizen
Ch.	Bench Show Champion
Dual Ch.	A dog that is both bench and field champion
FC	Field Champion
JH	Junior Hunter
MH	Master Hunter

OFA	The Orthopedic Foundation for Animals, 817 Virginia Avenue, Columbia, Mo. 65201. OFA has three veterinarians (each a radiologist, located in a different area of the country) examine the X-rays of a dog's hips and elbows. A consensus report is issued, and if it is favorable, the owner will receive a numbered certificate attesting that the dog has sound hips.
OTCH	Obedience Trial Champion
SH	Senior Hunter
TD	Tracking Dog
TDX	Tracking Dog Excellent
UD	Utility Dog—the highest Obedience title
UDT	Utility and Tracking Dog
WD	Working Dog—A title earned under the American Chesapeake Club regulations in which a dog retrieves game on both land and water.
WDX	Working Dog Excellent—Similar to WD except that the dog must be steady to shot and must retrieve doubles on land and water.
WDQ	Working Dog Qualified—The most advanced American Chesapeake Club title, requiring multiple marks and blind retrieves.

American Chesapeake Club Specialty Shows

BEST OF BREED

1926	Ch. BARRON'S LILY PAD	M. S. Barron
1933	Ch. BUD PARKER'S RIPPLE	A. A. Bliss
1934	CINNAMIN II	Mabel Ingalls
1935	Ch. FLOATING POWER	C. W. Berg
1936	DILWYNE BIRD	Dilwyne Kennels
1937	DIXIANNA	A. A. Bliss
1938	SHINNECOCK BELLE	Walter Roesler
1939	Ch. CINAR'S TWEED	Raymond Guest
1940	NATIVE SHORE MOLLIE	Helen Patterson
1941	NAPEAGUE NAUGHTY NANNETTE	Mary Neill
1942–1945	*NO SHOWS HELD*	
1946	Ch. CINDY of GREENRIDGE	Mrs. A. W. Owens, Jr.
1947–1953	*NO SHOWS HELD*	
1954	Ch. WIL-DA'S DRAKE, CDX	L. Wilson Davis
1955	Ch. CHESAPEAKE TIMBER	Charles Upham
1956	Ch. JODRI'S CATAMARAN, UD	Mrs. Charles Underwood
1957	Ch. ALPINE BIG BUTCH	Jack Woodall
1958	*NO SHOW HELD*	

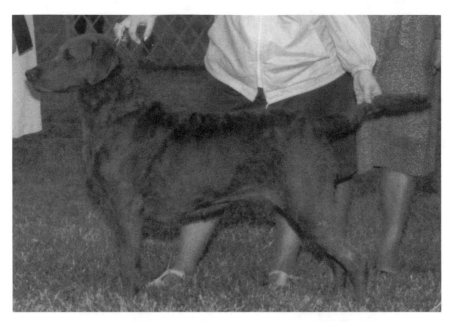

Am. & Can. Ch. Limefield Magnolia was Best of Breed ACC Specialty in 1984, under Anne Rogers Clark, with handler Jody M. Thomas. "Maggie" was bred by Betsy Humer, and was the foundation bitch for Marie Bonadies's Limefield Kennels.

1959	Ch. WEST RIVER RIPPLE	Eugene V. Weems
1960	Ch. THE PORT of WINDY BAY	Isabelle Bushkoff
1960 (#2)	Ch. PLATTE RIVER JANE	Mrs. Walter Heller
1961	Ch. WEST RIVER RIPPLE	Eugene V. Weems
1962	Ch. WEST RIVER RIPPLE	Eugene V. Weems
1963	Ch. KENSINGTON BIG BROWN	Nathaniel Hurwitz
1964	Ch. EASTERN WATERS' BARONESSA	Janet Horn
1965	Ch. EASTERN WATERS' BARONESSA	Janet Horn
1966	Ch. EASTERN WATERS' BARONESSA	Janet Horn
1967	Ch. NATIVE SHORE JUMBO BELLE	Kenneth Krueger
1968	EASTERN WATERS' OAK	Rupert & Elizabeth Humer
1969	Ch. LADY GINGER of HAMPTON COURT	Salvatore Miceli
1970	Ch. EASTERN WATERS' BROWN CHARGER, CD	Dr. Daniel Horn

Am. & Bda. Ch. Eastern Waters' Brown Charger, Am/Bda CD. Best of Breed, ACC Specialty Show 1970, judge Maxwell Riddle. Owner-handler: Dan Horn. "Charlie" was from the litter bred and raised by 14-year-old Marguerite Horn for her 4-H project. His record of 126 Bests of Breed and 29 Sporting Group placements topped the breed for several years.

1971	Ch. EASTERN WATERS' BIG GUNPOWDER	William K. Boyson
1972	CHESARAB'S LITTLE ACORN	Sheila DiVaccaro
1973	COLEWOOD'S the INNKEEPER	Richard Cole
1974	Ch. SALTY BOMARC	Dr. & Mrs. Marston Jones
1975	Ch. EASTERN WATERS' OAK, CD, WD	Rupert & Elizabeth Humer
1976	Ch. ASHBY'S CHOCOLATE CHIP	John & Christine DeVries
1977	Ch. TEAL'S TIGER	Susan Hatfield
1978	Ch. LONGCOVE'S GOLDEN GEMINI	Alfred & Jeannie Kinney
1979	Ch. REDLION'S J J SAMPLE	Jane Pappler

Ch. Chestnut Hills Stone E's Tug, Best of Breed, ACC Specialty Show 1991. Judge: Sue Cogley. Tug is bred and owned by Karen and Ron Anderson, always handled by Karen. This was Tug's third ACC Specialty Best of Breed. He won in 1985 from the classes, and in 1990 and in 1991. In 1991 Tug went Best of Breed from the classes at the Chesapeake Bay Retriever Club of Canada National Specialty Show, and became the only Chesapeake to win Best in National Specialty Shows in two countries.

1980	Ch. WYNDHAM'S ALGONQUIN	Helen Szostak & E. J. Atkins
1981	Ch. SNOCREE'S DAISY CLOVER	Carolyn Harris
1982	Ch. HEIR of ALNWICK CASTLE	Michael & Susan LaMielle
1983	Ch. STONEYCREEK HOPSCOTCH	Kellie Lewis & Susan Steuben
1984	Ch. LIMEFIELD MAGNOLIA	Marie Whitney Bonadies
1985	CHESTNUT HILLS STONE E'S TUG	Karen & Ronald Anderson
1986	Ch. SNOCREE'S & HI-HO'S BOOMERANG	E. Cottingham & L. Walden
1987	Ch. EASTERN WATERS' BREAK O'DAY, CD	Mrs. Daniel Horn

1988	Ch. EASTERN WATERS' DIAMOND DUST	Sarah Horn
1989	Ch. CHESTNUT HILLS STONE E'S BRU	Stephanie & Peter Jones
1990	Ch. CHESTNUT HILLS STONE E'S TUG	Karen & Ronald Anderson
1991	Ch. CHESTNUT HILLS STONE E'S TUG	Karen & Ronald Anderson
1992	Ch. FITZHUGH'S BAG the LIMIT	Meghan & Medelyn Conner and Darren Sausser
1993	Ch. COCO'S CHOCOLATE SENSATION	Sandra & Steven Dietrich

ISBN 0-87605-099-2